Spiralizer Cookbook: 103 Amazing and Absolutely Delicious Recipes

By

Stephanie N. Collins

Table of Contents

Introduction

Spiralizer is a perfect combination to live a healthy lifestyle. It is more natural and does not include many of the chemical processes that food undergoes compared to what we more commonly do today

So, what is a spiralizer? It is a kitchen tool that shreds food into strands and forms pastas and noodles. Vegetables are usually shredded through this tool but fruits can also be used with it.

The two basic types available are: the Paderno Spiralizers and Veggetti-style Spiralizers.

The **Veggetti-style** is a very inventive, easy to use, easy to clean and lightweight spiralizer that you can carry even when travelling. It is hand-held and looks like a pencil sharpener that is large enough to fit in a carrot or zucchini so there's always a way for you to prepare your favorite "pasta veggies" wherever you go.

The **Paderno style,** on the other hand, is a type of spiralizer that is a lot bigger and more versatile. It is a slicer that is hand powered, meaning it's neither electrical or battery operated. It's about the size of a counter top regular mixer, has more blades but it's safe because the veggies are inserted in the machine and directed towards the cutting blades.

Most Paderno-style Spiralizers come with three different blades, each of which spiralize your food differently.

- A noodle blade (Blade C) — for spaghetti-sized noodles

- A spiral blade (Blade B) — for thicker, curly noodles or curly fries

- A ribbon blade (Blade A) — a straight blade for ribbon cuts

Use the thinner noodle blade and make *Italian pasta dishes* with: parsnips, potatoes, turnips / kohlrabi / rutabagas, sweet potatoes, zucchini.

Use the thicker blade to create *veggie fries* with: carrots, jicama, potatoes, sweet potatoes, turnips / kohlrabi / rutabagas, zucchini.

Use the ribbon blade to create *wide ribbons, fine slices or half moons* with: apples, zucchini, cucumbers, sweet potatoes.

To create *rice-like veggie noodles,* you have to start by spiralizing vegetables. Once you have spiralized veggies, place them in a food processor and pulse for a few seconds. Once the vegetables resemble rice, you're done.

All vegetables can be "riced" except for cucumbers — their water content is just too high. Fruits can't be "riced" either.

The Paderno-style Spiralizers are very simple to use.

- Place the vegetable into the prongs and line it up with the de-seeing hole on the other side. The bottom of the spiralizer has nifty suction cups — don't forget to use them so it doesn't slide around!

- Spiralize by turning the crank. As you turn the crank, the item moves against the blades as the center moves through the hole (sort of like a pencil in a pencil sharpener).

TIP: After you make the noodles, some of them will be extremely long, so you can cut them with scissors.

These veggie noodles can be baked, boiled or roasted to create all kinds of dishes.

The art of spiralizing is versatile. It can be used for all ages, skill levels and even diet lifestyles. It allows you to transform simple foods into something extraordinary, healthy and nutritious and one good thing about it – the recipes are truly easy to make!

Sweet Potato Zoodles with Creamy Spinach-Cashew Sauce

Prep time: 2 hours

Cook time: 25 minutes

Serves: 4 to 6

Ingredients:

- ¾ cup of water

- 1 cup of cashews

- 1 tablespoon of oil

- 4 large spiralized sweet potatoes

- 1 garlic clove

- ½ teaspoon of salt

- 2 cups of baby spinach

- Pepper and salt, to taste

- Olive oil, for drizzling

- Handful of fresh herbs (chives, basil leaves, etc.)

Directions:

1. Soak cashew nuts with water in your bowl for about 2 hours or more.

2. Drain, then rinse completely. Place the garlic, cashews, water, and salt in a blender and blend until smooth.

3. Heat the oil in a large skillet, over medium heat. Add in sweet potatoes then cook for around 6 to 7 minutes until it becomes tender and crisp. Remove from the heat, then add spinach until wilted.

4. Add half the fresh herbs, then half of the creamy sauce to the pan. Toss well until thoroughly combined. If the mixture becomes very sticky, add more water. Season with pepper and salt. Drizzle with the olive oil, then top it with the remaining fresh herbs. Serve and enjoy!

Nutrition facts: 369 calories; 45.1g carbs; 18.5g fats; 6.6g fiber; 9.4g protein; 9.1g sugar.

Zucchini Pasta with Chorizo, Shrimp, Corn and Saffron

Prep time: 3 minutes

Cook time: 8 minutes

Serves: 2

Ingredients:

- 3 zucchinis, peeled and spiralized
- 1 chorizo (sliced to half inch pieces)
- 1 minced garlic clove
- 6 shrimp (deveined and peeled)
- ⅓ cup of veggie broth
- 1 tablespoon of parsley (chopped)
- 4 saffron threads
- 1 ear of corn
- 1 teaspoon of powdered chili
- Pepper and salt, to taste

Directions:

1. Using a medium saucepan, put in the corn and cover with water then boil. Let it cook for about 2 minutes or until the corn is cooked. Scrape the kernels and place them in the bowl. Add in the powdered chili, then mix well. Set aside.

2. Heat a large skillet over medium heat. Add the chorizo and cook for about 2 minutes, then flip on the other side. Add garlic and keep on sautéing for 1 minute more. Do not burn the garlic. Set aside.

3. Meanwhile, season shrimp with salt & pepper and then add to the pan. Cook for a minute per side. Add the veggie broth, corn, zucchini pasta, and saffron. Mix well and cook for around 3 minutes or until the zucchini softens and is completely heated.

4. Transfer to a plate, garnish with parsley then serve.

Nutrition facts: 224 calories; 13.75g fats; 23.7g carbs; 16.75g protein.

Greek Spiralized Cucumber Noodles

Prep time: 15 minutes

Serves: 2 to 4

Ingredients:

- 1 cup of grape tomatoes, halved

- 2 seedless cucumbers, spiralized

- ¼ of red onion, sliced thinly

- ⅓ cup of kalamata olives, pitted and chopped

- ½ cup of crumbled Feta cheese

- Pepper and salt, to taste

- 4 tablespoons of hummus

Directions:

1. Divide spiralized cucumbers into plates, then top with olives, red onions, and tomatoes.

2. Add spoonfuls of hummus at the center of the cucumber noodles. Sprinkle feta cheese on top and season with pepper and salt. Serve.

Nutrition facts: 118 calories; 6.8g fats; 11.1g carbs; 5.3g protein; 4.6g sugar; 2.6g fiber.

Inspiralized Chicken Bruschetta

Prep time: 2 hours to 24 hours for marinating

Cook time: 25 minutes

Serves: 4

Ingredients:

- 4 chicken breasts (boneless and skinless)

- 2 large zucchini, spiralized

- 1½ cups of chopped tomatoes

- 2 minced garlic cloves

- 2 tablespoons of olive oil

- 3 tablespoons basil leaves, chopped

- Store bought Italian dressing (1 cup + 2 tablespoons)

- Pepper and salt, to taste

Directions:

1. Marinate the chicken in advance. Place the chicken in a ziplock bag. Add 1 cup of Italian dressing to the Ziplock bag. Mix the marinade so it covers the chicken. Place in a fridge and marinate the chicken for about 2 hours or overnight.

2. Make the bruschetta topping in advance. Combine garlic, tomatoes, basil leaves, and the remaining Italian dressing. Season with pepper and salt. Cover, then refrigerate for about 2 hours or overnight as well.

3. Using a large-sized skillet, heat a tablespoon of olive oil over medium heat, then cook marinated chicken breasts for around 15 minutes, flipping halfway through cooking. Make sure that both sides are browned and completely cooked. Remove from the pan.

4. Using the same pan, add the rest of the olive oil then add zucchini, and 2 tablespoons of the bruschetta topping. Cook for about 5 to 6 minutes, occasionally stirring the noodles. Once all liquid is absorbed, remove from heat, then transfer to plate. Place chicken on top, then put the remaining bruschetta mixture on top of each chicken. Serve.

Nutrition facts: 276 calories; 17g fats; 11g carbs; 25.3g protein; 7g sugar; 2g fiber.

Spiralized Sweet Potato Fries

Prep time: 10 minutes

Cook time: 30 minutes

Serves: 1 to 2

Ingredients:

- 1 large sized sweet potato, spiralized

- 2 tablespoons of olive oil or use canola oil

- ½ teaspoon of salt

- ½ teaspoon of powdered garlic

- ¼ teaspoon of cayenne pepper

Directions:

1. Preheat your oven to 450°F.

2. Toss the spiralized sweet potatoes with oil and all seasonings using a ziplock bag, until it is coated evenly.

3. Spread the sweet potatoes on a lined baking pan (do not overcrowd). Bake for around 20 to 25 minutes on the top of the rack, turning once to avoid burning. Serve hot.

Nutrition facts: 204 calories; 14.2g fats; 19.3g carbs; 2g protein; 6g sugar; 3.1g fiber.

Pear Spiralized Noodles with Yogurt Parfait

Prep time: 5 minutes

Cook time: 5 minutes

Serves: 1

Ingredients:

- Greek yogurt (any flavor of your preference)

- 2 medium pears

- ¾ cup of diced fruits (mix of strawberries, bananas and blueberries)

- 1 cup of your favorite granola

Directions:

1. Create pear noodles.

2. Divide the mixed diced fruits among 3 separate mason jars. Top it with the yogurt then put ⅓ cup of granola into each jar.

3. Top the granola with the pear noodles. Serve and enjoy. You can also chill first before serving.

Nutrition facts: 255 calories; 2.3g fats; 51g carbs; 10.3g protein; 22.4g sugar; 7.6g fiber.

Chicken and Spiralized Zucchini Noodle Soup

Prep time: 15 minutes

Cook time: 3 to 4 hours on high or 7 to 8 hours on low (slow cooker)

Serves: 8

Ingredients:

- 1 lb chicken breasts (skinless and boneless; halved)

- 6 cups of chicken broth (less-sodium)

- ¼ teaspoon of pepper and salt

- 2 teaspoons of garlic (chopped)

- ½ cup of carrots (chopped)

- 2 teaspoons of Italian seasoning

- ½ cup of onion (chopped)

- ½ cup of celery (chopped)

- 2 bay leaves

- ¼ teaspoon of thyme (dried)

- ½ teaspoon of powdered onion

- 2 medium-size zucchini (spiralized)

Directions:

1. Put chicken in the slow cooker and season with pepper and salt. Place all the ingredients as well, except the spiralized zucchini. Combine well.Cover, then cook for 3 to 4 hours on high or 7 to 8 hours on low. Remove bay leaves.

2. Add in the zucchini noodles, cover and cook for another 10 minutes or until noodles have softened a bit. Serve.

Nutrition facts: 98 calories; 2g fats; 5g carbs; 14.5g protein; 2.5g sugar; 1g fiber.

Butternut Squash and Beets Noodle

Prep time: 10 minutes

Cook time: 15 minutes

Serves: 4

Ingredients:

- 1 medium-sized beet (peeled)

- 1 medium-sized golden beet (peeled)

- 1 small butternut squash (peeled)

- 1 tablespoon of olive oil (plus 2 teaspoons more)

- ½ cup of Italian parsley (divided)

- Zest of a lemon

- 1 oz crumbled feta cheese

- ⅓ teaspoon of kosher salt

- ½ teaspoon of pepper

Directions:

1. Spiralize the beets and butternut squash.

2. Combine all the veggies and a small amount of water in a microwaveable bowl. Microwave them for about a minute or until veggies become tender. Drain veggie noodles using paper towel.

3. Add a tablespoon of olive oil, parsley, lemon zest, pepper, and salt.Using a food processor or blender, blend well until it becomes smooth.

4. Once done, add the pesto sauce in the veggie noodles, then toss gently to combine. Sprinkle feta cheese on top. Serve.

Nutrition facts: 114 calories; 7.3g fats; 11g carbs; 2g protein; 3g fiber.

Spiralized Hash Browns

Prep time: 10 minutes

Cook time: 10 minutes

Serves: 4

Ingredients:

- 12 oz of Yukon Gold potatoes, spiralized

- ½ teaspoon of kosher salt

- 2 tablespoons of canola oil

- 1½ teaspoons of cornstarch

- Cooking spray

Directions:

1. Squeeze the excess moisture out of the spiralized potatoes using paper towel, then sprinkle with salt and cornstarch. Lightly toss to coat evenly.

2. Heat the oil in a large non-stick pan, over medium heat, then swirl to fully coat pan. Place 4 noodle piles on the pan. Cook for around 4 to 5 minutes or until crisp and golden brown. Spray the top of the potato with cooking spray then flip. Cook again for another 3 to 4 minutes until golden brown. Serve.

Nutrition facts: 122 calories; 7g fats; 15g carbs; 1g protein; 2g fiber.

Parsnip Pasta Puttanesca

Prep time: 30 minutes

Cook time: 40 minutes

Serves: 4

Ingredients:

- 4 parsnips, spiralized

- 1 onion, diced

- 3 garlic cloves, diced

- 1 teaspoon of red chili flakes

- 4 anchovy fillets

- 1 cup of tomatoes, diced

- 1 tablespoon of capers, diced

- ¼ teaspoon of salt

- 1 handful of flat-leaf parsley

- Black pepper, to season

- 1 tablespoon coconut oil

- 4 tablespoons olives, chopped

Directions:

1. Add coconut oil to the large, non-stick skillet and melt it over medium heat. Cook the spiralized parsnips for about 20 minutes or until softened. Set aside on a plate.

2. Using the same skillet, cook the onion and garlic until soft and translucent, occasionally stirring.

3. Add in the capers, anchovies, and olives, and stir them into the onions and garlic. Mix in the tomatoes, chili flakes, and salt, then stir until well combined.

4. Mix in the parsnip pasta and season with salt, then toss to combine.

5. Sprinkle with fresh parsley and black pepper on top. Serve.

Nutrition facts: 208 calories; 17g fats; 15g carbs; 4.5g protein; 6g fiber.

Baked Spiralized Zucchini with Quinoa

Prep time: 10 minutes

Cook time: 30 minutes

Serves: 4

Ingredients:

- 4 cups of spiralized zucchini

- 8 oz of cheddar cheese (shredded)

- 2 tablespoons of EVOO (extra virgin olive oil)

- 1 cup of quinoa (cooked)

- 2 tablespoons of parmesan cheese (grated)

- ½ teaspoon of salt

Directions:

1. Preheat your oven to 400°F.

2. In a medium-sized bowl, toss the zucchini, quinoa, salt, oil, and cheddar cheese. Place in a baking dish, then sprinkle parmesan cheese on top.

3. Bake for about 30 minutes or until golden. Serve.

Nutrition facts: 246 calories; 17.4g fats; 14.1g carbs; 10.8g protein; 2.2g fiber; 4.7g sugar.

Eggplant Noodles with Pasta Primavera Sauce

Prep time: 20 minutes

Cook time: 30 minutes

Serves: 3

Ingredients:

- 2 medium-sized eggplant, spiralized

- 2 tablespoons of coconut oil

- 1 tablespoon of garlic, minced

- ½ cup of red onion, chopped

- ½ medium red pepper

- 1½ cups of crimini mushrooms, sliced

- 2 carrots, spiralized

- 1 large tomato, chopped

- ½ cup of frozen green peas, rinsed and drained

- ½ cup of kale, chopped

- ½ cup of water

- 1 bay leaf

- ½ cup of almond milk

- 1 tablespoon of arrowroot

- 1½ teaspoons of sea salt

- ¼ teaspoon of red pepper flakes

- 1 teaspoon of Italian seasoning

- Fresh parsley, to garnish

- Parmesan cheese, to top

Directions:

1. Toss the eggplant noodles with 1 teaspoon of salt and place them in a sieve over a bowl. Allow them to "sweat" for 20 minutes before placing them in a cotton dishtowel to squeeze out the excess moisture. Melt 1 tablespoon coconut oil in a skillet, sauté the eggplant noodles for 5 minutes, set aside.

2. Heat remaining coconut oil over medium heat and add in the onion and bell pepper. Sauté for a few minutes before adding the mushrooms and garlic. Cook for about 5 minutes or until the water from the mushroom evaporates. Mix in the tomato, salt, herb blend, and red pepper flakes and cook for 1-2 minutes. Pour in the water and add the bay leaf, then let it simmer for another 1-2 minutes.

3. Meanwhile, in a separate cup, whisk the milk and arrowroot. Pour this mixture into the pan.

4. Add in the peas and kale and combine everything well. Let the sauce thicken before removing from heat.

5. Pour the sauce on top of the eggplant noodles with the spiraled carrots and top with parsley. Sprinkle the top with parmesan cheese. Serve.

Nutrition facts: 290 calories; 15.3g fats; 36.9g carbs; 7.4g protein; 15g fiber.

Tuna Casserole

Prep time: 20 minutes

Cook time: 60 minutes

Serves: 4

Ingredients:

- 2 cans of tuna fish (about 5 oz each)

- 2 zucchinis, spiralized

- 1 small onion, chopped

- 3 garlic cloves, finely minced

- 1 stalk of celery, chopped

- 3 tablespoons of ghee

- 1 tablespoon of arrowroot powder

- 1½ cups of almond milk

- Pink salt, to taste

- Fresh black pepper, cracked, to taste

Directions:

1. Preheat the oven to 350°F.

2. In a pan, sauté the onion, garlic, and celery in 1 tablespoon of ghee and season with pink salt and freshly cracked black peppers, until veggies are golden.

3. In a separate pan, over medium-low heat, make a roux by combining and mixing together 2 tablespoons of ghee and 1 tablespoon of arrowroot. Cook until thick and bubbly. Season with salt and pepper to taste. Pour in the almond milk and slowly whisk it into the mixture.

4. Place the tuna in a casserole dish, and mash it with a fork. Add in the spiralized zucchinis and layer them out evenly. Pour in the roux mixture and spread evenly. Then bake it for about 45minutes to 1 hour. Serve.

Nutrition facts: 246 calories; 17.4g fats; 14.1g carbs; 15.8g protein; 2.2g fiber; 4.7g sugar.

Chow Mein

Prep time: 10 minutes

Cook time: 30 minutes

Serves: 2

Ingredients:

- ½ pound of chicken, cut into 1-in. strips

- ½ tablespoon of ghee

- 1 tablespoon of coconut aminos

- 1 tablespoon of rice vinegar

- ½ green cabbage, cored and thinly sliced

- 1 large carrot, shredded

- 1 small broccoli, stemmed and cut into bite-size pieces

- 2 zucchinis, spiraled

Sauce:

- 3 tablespoons of coconut aminos

- 2 tablespoons of rice vinegar

- 1 teaspoon of sesame oil

- 1 tablespoon of fish sauce

- 2-inch ginger, fresh, minced

- 2 cloves of garlic, minced

- 1 teaspoon of honey

- ¼ teaspoon sriracha sauce

Directions:

1. In a large wok, over medium-high heat, melt the ghee. Add in the chicken, 1 tablespoon of coconut aminos, and 1 tablespoon of rice vinegar. Stir all together and cook for 5-7 minutes.

2. In large-sized bowl, whisk together all the sauce ingredients. Add the cabbage, carrot, and broccoli into the sauce and toss until well covered.

3. Mix all these into the wok and stir. Cover and cook for another 10-15 minutes or until the cabbage is wilted. Stir often.

4. Add in the zucchini noodles and allow to cook for another 7-10 minutes. Serve.

Nutrition facts: 202 calories; 10.4g fats; 11.1g carbs; 10.8g protein; 3.2g fiber.

Spriralized Zucchini Stir Fry

Prep time: 10 minutes

Cook time: 10 minutes

Serves: 4

Ingredients:

- 2 tablespoons of veggie oil

- 2 spiralized yellow onions

- 1 tablespoon of soy sauce

- 1 tablespoon of sesame seeds

- 2 tablespoons of teriyaki sauce

- 4 small sized spiralized zucchini

Directions:

1. Heat oil in the wok over medium heat and then add in onions. Cook for around 4 to 5 minutes or until tender.

2. Add zucchini, then cook for another 2 minutes. Add in soy sauce, sesame seeds and teriyaki sauce and cook for another 5 minutes more. Serve.

Nutrition facts: 116 calories; 8.2g fats; 2.7g protein; 2.4g fiber.

Bacon and Basil Zucchini Pasta

Prep time: 10 minutes

Cook time: 30 minutes

Serves: 4

Ingredients:

- 4 medium zucchinis, spiralized

- 2 tablespoons of olive oil

- 1 clove of crushed garlic

- ¾ cup of sun dried tomatoes in olive oil, sliced

- ¼ cup of fresh basil, chopped

- 6 slices of bacon, trimmed of fat and thinly sliced

- 1 small chile, chopped finely

- 1 tablespoon of pine nuts

Directions:

1. Heat 1 tablespoon olive oil in a pan over high heat and cook zucchini for about 3 minutes. Add in the sliced bacon and cook for a minute or two or until cooked. Reduce the heat.

2. Add tomatoes, garlic, pine nuts, chile and additional oil in the pan. Toss to combine well, sauté for a few minutes, then remove from heat. Transfer to the plate, sprinkle with chopped fresh basil.

Nutrition facts: 208 calories; 17g fats; 3g carbs; 9.5g protein; 2g fiber; 3g sugar.

Beet Noodles with Cherry Tomatoes and Bacon

Prep time: 15 minutes

Cook time: 20 minutes

Serves: 2

Ingredients:

- 1 large beet, spiralized

- 3 to 4 strips of bacon

- Salt and pepper, to taste

- ½ cup of cherry tomatoes

- 1 garlic clove, minced

- 2-3 tablespoons of feta cheese, crumbled

- 1 tablespoon of fresh parsley, chopped

- Cooking spray

Directions:

1. Heat pan over medium heat, then coat with cooking spray. Cook bacon strips until crisp for around 7 minutes, then crumble and set aside.

2. Remove half of the bacon fat from the pan and add in the beets. Toss and cook for about a minute or until the noodles start to wilt.

3. Add in garlic, tomatoes, pepper and salt, then let cook for around 5 to 7 minutes.

4. Transfer to plate, then top with crumbled bacon, parsley and feta cheese. Serve.

Nutrition facts: 138 calories; 8g fats; 29g carbs; 8g protein; 2g fiber; 5g sugar.

Zucchini Caprese Salad

Prep time: 15 minutes

Cook time: 15 minutes

Serves: 8

Ingredients:

- 8 cups of spiralized zucchini

- 8 oz of mozzarella pearls

- 1 oz of chopped fresh basil

- 4 oz of cherry tomatoes

For the dressing:

- ¼ cup of EVOO (extra virgin olive oil)

- 1 tablespoon of lemon juice (fresh)

- 3 tablespoons of red wine vinegar

- ¼ teaspoon of garlic powder

- Pepper and salt, to taste

Directions:

1. In a large bowl, combine zucchini noodles, tomatoes, mozzarella, and chopped basil.

2. In another bowl, combine dressing ingredients and whisk. Toss them together. Serve.

Nutrition facts: 152 calories; 11.7g fats; 6.3g carbs; 8.4g protein; 1.4g fiber; 3.7g sugar.

Chicken and Veggie Lo Mein

Prep time: 10 minutes

Cook time: 20 minutes

Serves: 6

Ingredients:

- 1½ lbs of chicken (boneless and sliced thinly)

- 2 teaspoons of grated ginger

- 4 tablespoons of avocado oil

- 1 tablespoon of soy sauce

- 3 garlic cloves, minced

- 4 oz of onions, sliced

- 7 oz of shitake mushrooms, sliced

- 4 oz of carrots, sliced

- 2 spiralized zucchini

- Pepper and salt, to taste

For the sauce:

- 1 tablespoon of rice wine vinegar

- 2 tablespoons of oyster sauce

- 1 tablespoon of stevia sweetener

- 2 tablespoons of soy sauce

Directions:

1. Heat 2 tablespoons avocado oil and cook chicken over medium heat. As you cook chicken halfway, add in garlic, ginger and soy sauce. When chicken is no longer pink, turn off heat.

2. In another large pan, add 2 tablespoons avocado oil, carrots, mushrooms and onion. Cook until tender, then toss the zucchini. Season to taste.

3. Meanwhile, whisk all the ingredients for the sauce. Mix in with the veggies on the pan, then add in the chicken. Serve.

Nutrition facts: 209 calories; 10.9g fats; 5.7g carbs; 24.2g protein; 0.7g fiber; 2.6g sugar.

Sriracha and Garlic Hash Browns

Prep time: 10 minutes

Cook time: 20 minutes

Serves: 2

Ingredients:

- 1-2 tablespoons of garlic, minced

- 1 large size yam, spiralized (you can use sweet potato as substitute)

- 2 teaspoons of sriracha sauce

- 1 tablespoon of EVOO (extra virgin olive oil)

- Pepper and salt, to taste

Directions:

1. Cut the spiralized yams a few times.

2. In a saucepan, heat oil over medium heat, then add minced garlic, spiralized yam, pepper, salt, and sriracha. Sautee for about 5 to 10 minutes until yam is cooked through. Press down the yams to brown them for around 1 to 2 minutes. Transfer to plate and serve with baked eggs, if desired. Enjoy!

Nutrition facts: 192 calories; 7g fats; 31g carbs; 2g protein; 2g fiber; 2g sugar.

Yellow Squash Zoodle with Garlic Shrimp

Prep time: 10 minutes

Cook time: 20 minutes

Serves: 2

Ingredients:

- 1 celeriac root, peeled and spiralized

- 4 yellow squash, peeled and spiralized

- 3 garlic cloves, minced

- ½ diced yellow onion

- 10 cherry tomatoes

- 1 tablespoon of EVOO (extra virgin olive oil)

- 2 tablespoons of fresh dill

- ½ of lemon juiced

- Pepper and salt, to taste

- ½ teaspoon of red pepper, crushed

- ½ cup of water

- 1 lb of shrimp, peeled and deveined

Directions:

1. In a large skillet, heat olive oil, then sauté garlic, squash, celery root, pepper, salt, and onion for 3 minutes.

2. Add in the shrimp, tomatoes, water, lemon juice, and red pepper. Continue cooking for another 3 to 5 minutes more. Serve and top with dill.

Nutrition facts: 444 calories; 14g fats; 29g carbs; 52g protein; 6g fiber.

Beef Stroganoff with Spiralized Potato Noodles

Prep time: 10 minutes

Cook time: 25 minutes

Serves: 2

Ingredients:

- ¾ lb of lean beef, chopped into bite size pieces

- 2 white potatoes, peeled and spiralized (Blade A, to create wider noodle)

- 2 sweet potatoes, peeled and spiralized (Blade A, to create wider noodle)

- 1 punnet of mushrooms, (stems trimmed, washed well and sliced)

- ½ of yellow onion, sliced

- ½cup of red wine

- ½ can of coconut milk

- 2 teaspoons of fresh thyme

- 1 tablespoon of minced garlic

- Pepper and salt, to taste

- 2 tablespoons of olive oil

Directions:

1. In a large skillet, heat the oil, then brown beef with the onion. Add in the rest of the ingredients and continue cooking over medium heat, for around 8 to 10 minutes or until the veggie noodles are cooked. Serve hot and enjoy!

Nutrition facts: 569 calories; 17g fats; 61g carbs; 33g protein; 7g fiber.

Beet and Cucumber Salad with Feta and Mint

Prep time: 15 minutes

Cook time: 15 minutes

Serves: 2

Ingredients:

- 4 beets, peeled and spiralized

- 3 cucumbers, peeled and spiralized

- 1 tablespoon of EVOO (extra virgin olive oil)

- 2 tablespoons of crumbled Feta cheese

- 10 diced mint leaves

- 4 tablespoons of prepared vinaigrette of your choice

- 8 spiced or candied walnuts

- Pepper and salt, to taste

Directions:

1. Preheat your oven to 400°F. Coat the beets with olive oil, season with pepper and salt, then bake for around 5 to 7 minutes or until cooked but firm. Let cool and set aside.

2. Place all the ingredients in a bowl including the baked beets then toss. Transfer to a plate and sprinkle with walnut pieces and feta cheese on top. Serve.

Nutrition facts: 439 calories; 19g fats; 31g carbs; 10g protein; 9g fiber.

Garden Veggie Noodle Salad

Prep time: 15 minutes

Cook time: 15 minutes

Serves: 2

Ingredients:

- 3 large peeled carrots, spiralized (follow the directions of your particular vegetable spiralizer)

- 2 peeled cucumbers, spiralized

- 1 peeled yellow squash, spiralized

- 2 peeled zucchinis, spiralized

- ½ of an avocado, sliced

- 1 large-sized tomato, sliced

- 4 tablespoons of store bought vinaigrette

- 2 tablespoons of crumbled blue cheese

- ¼ of sliced red onion

Directions:

1. Layer each of the spiralized veggies on a plate, one by one. Top each with tomato, onion, sliced avocado and blue cheese.

2. Top it with the vinaigrette. Serve.

Nutrition facts: 324 calories; 15g fats; 40g carbs; 12g protein; 12g fiber.

Spiralized Butternut Squash with Chicken and Peppers

Prep time: 10 minutes

Cook time: 20 minutes

Serves: 2

Ingredients:

- 1 sliced red pepper

- 1 butternut squash

- 2 cooked chicken breasts

- 1 cup of prepared marinara sauce

- 1 tablespoon of EVOO (extra virgin olive oil)

- Pepper and salt, to taste

- Fresh parsley for garnish

Directions:

1. Preheat your oven to 375°F.

2. Slice the top and bottom of the squash, then remove the seeds. Peel squash, cut to small sizes, then spiralize.

3. Place the squash noodles and red bell peppers on a baking tray and drizzle with EVOO. Season with pepper and salt and bake for around 9 to 10 minutes.

4. Transfer to a plate and top with grilled or baked chicken, marinara sauce and garnish with parsley. Serve.

Nutrition facts: 430 calories; 15g fats; 42g carbs; 39g protein; 9g fiber; 7g sugar.

Chicken Sausage with Spiralized Veggie

Prep time: 15 minutes

Cook time: 20 minutes

Serves: 2

Ingredients:

- 1 cup of crushed tomatoes, canned

- ½ teaspoon of Italian seasoning

- ½ teaspoon of garlic powder

- ½ teaspoon of onion powder

- 1 cup of sugar snap peas

- 14 oz of yellow squash, spiralized into noodles

- ½ cup of onion, sliced

- 6 oz of cooked Italian chicken sausage, sliced and halved

- 1 tablespoon of Parmesan cheese, grated

Directions:

1. Preheat your oven to 375°F, then line a baking tray with aluminum foil sprayed with nonstick spray.

2. Combine seasonings and crushed tomatoes. Lay spiralized squash, onion and snap peas on the baking tray. Top it with the chicken sausage and crushed tomato mixture. Sprinkle with cheese. Cover with another piece of aluminum foil, then seal the edges to form a packet.

3. Bake for around 20 minutes or until the veggies become tender. Open packet then transfer to plate or bowl. Serve.

Nutrition facts: 266 calories; 9.5g fats; 23.5g carbs; 23g protein; 6g fiber; 12.5g sugar.

Yummy Apple Pie Noodles

Prep time: 5 minutes

Cook time: 10 minutes

Serves: 2

Ingredients:

- 2 medium apples, peeled and spiralized into noodles

- 1 pack of sweetener, no-calorie

- ¼ teaspoon of vanilla extract

- ¼ teaspoon of cinnamon

- 1 tablespoon of cornstarch

- Dash of salt

- Whipped cream, optional

- Non-stick spray

Directions:

1. In a bowl, mix cornstarch with cold water until fully dissolved. Add in the sweetener, vanilla extract, cinnamon plus salt. Mix until combined well.

2. Add in the apple noodles, then toss to fully coat.

3. Heat pan over medium heat and spray some non-stick spray.

4. Add apple mix then cook, stirring occasionally, for around 3 to 4 minutes or until it becomes gooey and thick. Serve.

Nutrition facts: 101 calories; 0g fats; 26g carbs; 0.5g protein; 2.5g fiber; 17.5g sugar.

Tofu and Zucchini Salad

Prep time: 15 minutes

Cook time: 10 minutes

Serves: 2

Ingredients:

- 2 zucchinis, spiralized

- 1 cup of carrots, diced

- 1 block of cooked tofu, cubed

- ½ cup of pitted cherries, diced

- ½ of onion, diced

For the dressing:

- 1 tablespoon of tamari

- 1½ teaspoons of garlic

- 2 tablespoons of rice wine

- 1 teaspoon of ginger

- 1 tablespoon of sesame oil

- 1 tablespoon of peanut butter

Directions:

1. Place the zucchini noodles on two layers of paper towels, and squeeze out excess liquid.

2. Combine carrots, onions, and cherries in a bowl. Add in spiralized noodles and cooked tofu.

3. In a jar, mix all dressing ingredients. Combine well. Pour the dressing over the salad. Serve.

Nutrition facts: 393 calories; 18.4g fats; 43.8g carbs; 20g protein; 6.7g fiber; 13.2g sugar.

Parsnip Waffles

Prep time: 10 minutes

Cook time: 15 minutes

Serves: 2

Ingredients:

- 2 large parsnips, spiralized

- 1 large beaten egg

- ¼ teaspoon of garlic powder

- ½ tablespoon EVOO (extra virgin olive oil)

- 3 tablespoons of chives, chopped

- Pepper and salt, to taste

- ¼ cup of Greek yogurt (optional)

- 2 teaspoons of lemon juice (optional)

Directions:

1. Preheat your waffle iron.

2. Meanwhile, heat the oil in a large pan, then add parsnips. Season with pepper, salt and garlic powder. Cover, then cook around 5 minutes or until the noodles are cooked well and wilted.

3. Transfer to a bowl, then add chives and egg. Toss and combine well. Spray cooking spray on the waffle iron, then place the parsnip mixture. Cook to your waffle iron's settings. Once done, remove carefully and then transfer to plate.

4. Combine Greek yogurt with lemon juice, then add mixture on top, if desired. Serve.

Nutrition facts: 192 calories; 7g fats; 30g carbs; 5g protein; 8g fiber; 8g sugar.

Spiralized Zucchini Salad with Spinach and Avocado Dressing

Prep time: 10 minutes

Cook time: 10 minutes

Serves: 2

Ingredients:

- ½ cup of edamame, shelled

- 1½ cups of spiralized zucchini

- ½ cup of red bell pepper, chopped

- ½ cup of celery, sliced

- ½ cup of cherry tomatoes

- 2 tablespoons of olives, optional

- ¼ cup of feta cheese, optional

For the dressing:

- ½ of avocado

- ½ cup of spinach, packed

- 2 tablespoons of Greek yogurt

- 2 tablespoons of EVOO (extra virgin olive oil)

- Juice of a lemon

- Pepper and salt, to taste

Directions:

1. Mix all the dressing ingredients using a blender. Pour into the bottom of the 2 mason jars.

2. Add in the celery first then peppers, edamame, feta cheese, tomatoes, and olives – following that order.

3. Lastly, put the zucchini noodles. Cover, then refrigerate.

4. When ready to eat, shake jar well and pour on a plate. Enjoy!

Nutrition facts: 298 calories; 22.9g fats; 20.7g carbs; 11.5g protein; 8.6g fiber; 9.2g sugar.

Zoodles with Corn and Tomatoes

Prep time: 10 minutes

Cook time: 10 minutes

Serves: 4

Ingredients:

- 4 medium-sized zucchini, spiralized

- 2 ears of sweet corn (kernels removed from the cob)

- 1 dry punnet of halved cherry tomatoes

- ½ cup of basil leaves

- ½ cup of Parmesan cheese, shaved

For the dressing:

- ¼ cup of olive oil

- ¼ cup of grape seed oil or any light oil

- ¼ cup of champagne vinegar

- ¼ teaspoon of sugar

- ½ teaspoon of kosher salt

- 1 garlic clove, crushed

Directions:

1. Combine the corn, tomatoes and zucchini in a bowl. Set aside.

2. Add all dressing ingredients in a jar and mix well. Pour the dressing over the veggies and toss to coat well. Let stand for a few minutes to soften zoodles.

3. Transfer to plate, then top with cheese and basil. Serve.

Nutrition facts: 350 calories; 28.8g fats; 22.2g carbs; 5.3g protein; 4.1g fiber; 11g sugar.

Cucumber Noodle with Lemon Gremolata

Prep time: 10 minutes

Cook time: 10 minutes

Serves: 8

Ingredients:

- 3 cucumber, spiralized

- 1 cup of parsley, chopped

- 2 minced garlic cloves

- ¼ cup of EVOO(extra virgin olive oil)

- 1 lemon, zested

- 2 tablespoons of lemon juice

- 2 cups of cherry tomatoes, halved

- Pepper and salt, to taste

Directions:

1. In a large bowl, combine cucumber noodles, tomatoes, and parsley. In another bowl, combine the remaining ingredients and adjust taste, if needed.

2. Add in the cucumber mixture, then toss gently. Serve immediately or you can chill before eating.

Nutrition facts: 90 calories; 7.3g fats; 8.5g carbs; 1.4g protein; 1.5g fiber; 4.5g sugar.

Apple Noodle with Rhubarb Crisps

Prep time: 10 minutes

Cook time: 35 minutes

Serves: 4

Ingredients:

- 3 apples, spiralized

- 3 rhubarb stalks

- ½ cup of granola of your choice

- Honey for drizzling

Directions:

1. Preheat your oven to 350°F.

2. Slice the rhubarb stalks lengthwise, then cube it. Place in the bowl and add in the apple noodles. Toss lightly.

3. Place mixture on ramekins and pack until 3 quarters filled, leaving enough room for the granola. Drizzle with honey on top and bake for around 30 minutes. Remove from the oven, then top with granola, then bake again for another 5 minutes more. Once cooked, serve.

Nutrition facts: 125 calories; 3g fats; 24g carbs; 2g protein; 4g fiber; 18g sugar.

Chicken with Cashew and Pear Salad

Prep time: 5 minutes

Cook time: 15 minutes

Serves: 2

Ingredients:

- 2 chicken breasts, sliced thinly

- 1 tablespoon of EVOO(extra virgin olive oil)

- 2 celery stalks, thinly sliced

- ¼ cup of roasted cashews, chopped

- 1 medium pear, spiralized

- ¼ cup of cilantro leaves

- Pepper and salt, to taste

For the dressing:

- 3 tablespoons of lime juice

- 2 scallions, sliced thinly

- 2 tablespoons of rice wine vinegar

- ½ teaspoon of jalapeno, chopped finely

- 2 teaspoons of honey

- 1 teaspoon of ginger, grated

- Pepper and salt, to taste

Directions:

1. In a bowl, place all dressing ingredients and mix well. Set aside.

2. Season the chicken first, then cook on medium heat with olive oil for around 5 to 6 minutes, flipping halfway through, until the chicken is cooked and no longer pink.

3. Meanwhile, mix the rest of ingredients, except cashews, in a bowl and pour the dressing. Toss to combine well. Place chicken on a plate, then top with pear salad. Top it with the cashews. Serve.

Nutrition facts: 341 calories; 14g fats; 21g carbs; 34g protein; 4g fiber; 12g sugar.

Jicama Noodles and Tortilla Soup

Prep time: 20 minutes

Cook time: 20 minutes

Serves: 4 to 6

Ingredients:

- 1 minced garlic clove

- 1 large jalapeno, seeded and diced finely

- 1 diced onion

- 1 tablespoon of EVOO (extra virgin olive oil)

- 6 cups of veggie or chicken broth, low-sodium

- 1 teaspoon of ground chili powder

- 1 teaspoon of oregano flakes

- ¼ teaspoon of smoked paprika

- ½ teaspoon of ground cumin

- 1 avocado, pitted and sliced

- 14.5oz of canned diced tomatoes

- 14.5 oz of canned black beans, drained and rinsed

- 1 medium jicama, spiralized

- 1 cup of cilantro leaves, chopped

- Pepper and salt, to taste

- 1 tablespoon lime juice

Directions:

1. Heat olive oil in a saucepan, then cook onions for around 2 minutes. Once soft, add in the jalapeno and garlic, then cook for 1 more minute.

2. Pour in the chicken broth, beans and tomatoes, then bring to boil. Once boiling, simmer then lower heat. Add the rest of the ingredients except the jicama noodles, then cook for 2 to 3 minutes. Season with salt and pepper.

3. Ladle soup, then top with the jicama noodles. Serve.

Nutrition facts: 248 calories; 9g fats; 36g carbs; 9g protein; 13g fiber; 9g sugar.

Coconut Curry Soup with Sweet Potato Noodles

Prep Time: 10 minutes

Cook Time: 22 minutes

Serves: 4

Ingredients:

- 1 large sweet potato, spiralized

- 3 cloves garlic, minced

- 1 small white onion, diced

- 1 red bell pepper, cut into thin strips

- 1 tablespoon minced fresh ginger

- 2 tablespoons yellow curry powder

- 1 (13.5 oz) can coconut milk

- 3 cups low-sodium vegetable broth

- ½ cup frozen green peas

- Juice of ½ lime

Garnishes:

- Lime wedges

- Chopped cilantro leaves

Directions:

1. Preheat the oven to 425°F.

2. Arrange the potato noodles in a single layer on a rimmed baking sheet. Bake for 10 minutes.

3. Meanwhile, in a soup pot, sauté the diced onion in 3 tablespoons of water until tender, about 5-6 minutes. Add the garlic, curry powder, ginger, and red bell pepper and sauté 2 minutes more. Pour in the vegetable broth and coconut milk. Simmer over medium heat for 15-20 minutes.

4. Add the green peas and lime juice and stir to combine.

5. To serve: ladle soup into serving bowl and then top with sweet potato noodles. Garnish with cilantro and lime wedges, if desired.

Nutrition Facts: |268 calories; 18g fats; 29g carbs; 4g fiber; 7g sugar; 4g protein.

Sweet Potato Spaghetti with Mozzarella

Prep time: 15 minutes

Cook time: 55 minutes

Serves: 6

Ingredients:

- 2 medium sweet potatoes, spiralized

- 1 tablespoon of EVOO (extra virgin olive oil)

- 2 garlic cloves,minced

- 9 slices of fresh mozzarella cheese, ¼-inch slice

- 2 cups of basil leaves

- 28 oz of canned whole tomatoes, peeled

- Pepper and salt, to taste

Directions:

1. Preheat your oven for 400°F.

2. Place tomatoes in a food processor and pulse until they are chopped coarsely.

3. Heat oil in a large pan, then add sweet potato noodles. Season with pepper and salt and cook for around 15 minutes or until cooked through. Set aside.

4. Using the same pan, add garlic and cook until fragrant. Add in the tomatoes, then bring to boil. Lower heat and let cook until the sauce becomes thick, for around 12 to 15 minutes.

5. In a large bowl, add the sweet potato, cooked tomato sauce, basil, and half of the mozzarella. Toss to combine well. Transfer to a baking dish, then top it with the remaining cheese. Bake for around 25 minutes or until the cheese becomes golden. Serve.

Nutrition facts: 282 calories; 14g fats; 24g carbs; 16g protein; 7g fiber; 13g sugar.

Curried Rutabaga with Brussels Sprouts and Edamame

Prep time: 15 minutes

Cook time: 20 minutes

Serves: 4

Ingredients:

- 12 oz of Brussels sprouts, sliced

- 2 garlic cloves, minced

- 1 tablespoon of coconut oil

- 2 teaspoons of ginger, minced

- 3 teaspoons of Thai red curry paste

- 13.5 oz of coconut milk, light

- 3 diced scallions, white and green parts divided

- 1 medium rutabaga, spiralized (you can use sweet potato as substitute)

- 3 cups of veggie broth

- 1 cup of edamame, frozen

- Basil leaves or cilantro

Directions:

1. In a large skillet, heat the oil, over a medium-high heat,t hen add garlic, ginger, white part of the scallions and Brussels sprouts. Cook for around 2 minutes or until Brussels sprouts become bright green. Add in the curry paste, veggie broth and coconut milk and let boil.

2. Once boiling, add rutabaga noodles plus edamame, then reduce heat. Cover and cook for around 7 to 10 minutes or until rutabaga is tender. Garnish with green scallions, cilantro or basil and then serve.

Nutrition facts: 241 calories; 12g fats; 23g carbs; 9g protein; 8g fiber; 9g sugar.

Korean Beef with Spiralized Cucumbers

Prep time: 15 minutes

Cook time: 20 minutes

Serves: 4

Ingredients:

- 2 minced garlic cloves

- 1 lb of lean ground beef

- ½ cup of yellow onion, diced

- 3-4 tablespoons of soy sauce

- 1 teaspoon of grated ginger

- 1 teaspoon of sesame oil

- ½ teaspoon of red pepper flakes

- 1 teaspoon of coconut oil

- 4 scallions, diced and divided to green and white parts

- 2 daikon radishes, spiralized and peeled

- Pepper and salt, to taste

- 1 seedless cucumber, spiralized

- 2 tablespoons of gochujang sauce

- Sesame seeds for garnish

Directions:

1. Heat large pan over high heat and spray with non-stick spray. Cook ground beef for around 5-7 minutes or until brown. Add the garlic, ginger and onion, then season with salt and pepper. Cook for about a minute or until it becomes fragrant.

2. Add sesame oil, soy sauce plus red paper flakes and combine well. Cover, then simmer for around 10 minutes.

3. Make rice-like daikon noodles using a food processor. In a medium pan, heat coconut oil, then add the white part of scallions. Cook for around 5 minutes or until it becomes soft. Add in the daikon rice, then season with pepper and salt. Cook for 3 minutes or until it becomes soft.

4. Once done, transfer to bowls then top it with beef and gochujang sauce. Garnish with sesame seeds and green part of scallions, then top it with cucumber noodles. Serve.

Nutrition facts:249 calories; 11g fats; 11g carbs; 25g protein; 2g fiber; 5g sugar.

Cucumber Kimchi

Prep time: 30 minutes

Serves: 6

Ingredients:

- 1 seedless cucumber, spiralized

- 2 garlic cloves, minced

- 2 scallions, divided to green and white parts, chopped finely

- 1-inch piece of ginger, peeled and minced

- 1 teaspoon of Kosher salt

- 2 teaspoons of honey

- 1 tablespoon Korean chile powder

- ½ teaspoon of fish sauce

- 2 tablespoons of rice vinegar

Directions:

1. Place cucumbers in a bowl and add Kosher salt. Let it stand for around 30 minutes.

2. In another bowl, combine the rest of the ingredients. Drain the cucumber and add to the vinegar mixture. Cover, then refrigerate for around 12 hours before consuming. Enjoy!

Nutrition facts: 23 calories; 0g fats; 5g carbs; 0g protein; 0g fiber; 3g sugar.

Cucumber Noodles and Shrimp

Prep time: 20 minutes

Cook time: 5 minutes

Serves: 2

Ingredients:

- 1 large seedless cucumber, spiralized

- 3 tablespoons of minced mint

- ⅓ cup of red onion, diced

- 2 roma tomatoes, diced and seeded

- 2 tablespoons of minced parsley

- ½ teaspoon of paprika

- ⅓ cup of pitted kalamata olives, halved

- 8 shrimps, deveined and peeled

- ½ teaspoon of garlic powder

- 2 teaspoons of EVOO (extra virgin olive oil)

- Pepper and salt, to taste

For the dressing:

- 1 teaspoon of honey

- 2 tablespoons of tahini

- 1 garlic clove, minced

- 2 tablespoons of water

- 2 tablespoons of lemon juice

- Pepper and salt, to taste

Directions:

1. Put all the ingredients for the dressing in a food processor and blend until it becomes creamy. Adjust to taste, then set aside.

2. Pat dry spiralized cucumber noodles then place in a bowl. Add in mint, parsley, tomato and onion.

3. Season shrimp with garlic powder, pepper and salt. Heat oil in a pan, over medium heat, then cook shrimps for around 2 minutes on each side or until cooked thoroughly.

4. Transfer cucumber mixture to a plate, then top with the cooked shrimp and dressing. Sprinkle paprika and olives on top. Serve.

Nutrition facts: 320 calories; 22g fats; 20g carbs;11g protein; 2g fiber; 7g sugar.

Cucumber Noodles with Tuna and Avocado Salad

Prep time: 20 minutes

Serves: 4

Ingredients:

- 12 oz of canned tuna in water

- 1 ripe avocado, pitted and peeled

- 5 tablespoons of Greek yogurt

- 2 seedless cucumber, spiralized

- 1½ teaspoons of Dijon mustard

- Pepper and salt, to taste

Directions:

1. Place avocado in a bowl, then mash. Add the rest of the ingredients and season, according to preference.

2. Add the cucumber noodles and toss well. Serve.

Nutrition facts: 182 calories; 8g fats; 5g carbs; 23g protein; 2g fiber; 1g sugar.

Plantain Noodles with Chipotle and Greek Yogurt

Prep time: 10 minutes

Cook time: 25 minutes

Serves: 2

Ingredients:

- 1 tablespoon of coconut oil

- 1 ear of corn, shucked

- 2 medium plantains, peeled and spiralized

- 2 eggs

- 1 avocado, peeled and cubed

For the yogurt:

- 1 chipotle pepper in adobo sauce plus ½ teaspoon of sauce

- ¼ cup of non-fat Greek yogurt

- 1 tablespoon of lime juice

- Pepper and salt, to taste

Directions:

1. Heat the coconut oil in a large skillet over medium heat, then add plantains. Season with pepper and salt. Cover and cook for around 10 to 15 minutes, toss frequently to avoid burning. Noodles should turn deep yellow color.

2. Meanwhile, cook the corn in a pot with water. Drop the corn into a large pot filled with boiling salted water. Cover the pot and let the water return to a boil again, then turn off the heat and keep the pot covered. After about 5 minutes, remove corn and transfer to plate. Shave the kernels from the corn, using a sharp knife. Set aside.

3. Meanwhile, blend all chipotle yogurt dressing using a food processor until it becomes creamy.

4. Place the noodles in a bowl, then add the corn and avocado. Toss to combine well. Place the same skillet back over medium heat and crack in the eggs. Cook sunny side up or over easy, to your preference.

5. Transfer noodles in a plate, then top with the eggs and chipotle yogurt dressing. Serve.

Nutrition facts:487 calories; 22g fats; 69g carbs;12g protein; 11g fiber; 27g sugar.

Spiralized Red Potatoes with Chicken

Prep time: 15 minutes

Cook time: 30 minutes

Serves: 3

Ingredients:

- ½ tablespoon of EVOO(extra virgin olive oil)

- ½ thinly sliced yellow onion

- 1 lb of chicken breasts or thighs, boneless and skinless, cut into 2 inch pieces

- ¼ teaspoon of paprika

- 1 garlic clove, minced

- 1 red bell pepper, sliced thinly

- 1 large red potato, spiralized

- 1 cup of grape tomatoes, chopped and seeds removed

- ½ cup of chicken broth

- ½ teaspoon of thyme

- ¼ teaspoon of red pepper flakes

- 1½ tablespoons of minced parsley

- ½ cup of olives

- Pepper and salt, to taste

Directions:

1. Season chicken with pepper and salt. In a large sized Dutch oven, heat the oil over medium heat, add chicken and cook for around 5 minutes or until it becomes light brown. Add in the onion, paprika, and pepper and cook for another 2 to 3 minutes.

2. Add the broth, garlic, tomatoes, thyme, red pepper flakes, then season with pepper and salt. Bring to boil, then reduce heat. Cover and simmer for 5 more minutes, and then uncover. Add potato noodles, toss to combine. Cook for another 10 more minutes or until the chicken and potatoes are cooked.

3. Add the olives and garnish with parsley. Serve.

Nutrition facts:274 calories; 12g fats; 15g carbs; 26g protein; 3g fiber; 5g sugar.

Scrambled Tofu and Broccoli Noodles

Prep time: 10 minutes

Cook time: 15 minutes

Serves: 3

Ingredients:

- 2 stems of broccoli, spiralized

- 2 tablespoons of EVOO (extra virgin olive oil)

- 14 oz of tofu, extra-firm

- 2 garlic cloves, minced

- 1 teaspoon of cumin

- 1 red bell pepper, diced finely

- 1 teaspoon of turmeric

- 1 tablespoon of yeast flakes

- Pepper and salt, to taste

- ½ onion, diced

Directions:

1. Bring water to boil using a medium sized pot. Once boiled, add the broccoli noodles and cook for around 2 to 3 minutes or until it becomes al dente.

2. Meanwhile, smash the tofu with the folk, until it crumbles and pat dry to remove excess water. Set aside.

3. Heat a large pan over medium heat, then add in olive oil. Add in garlic, onion and peppers and cook for about 3 to 5 minutes or until soft. Add cumin, then stir for about a minute, then add in the broccoli noodles, turmeric, tofu and yeast flakes. Season with pepper and salt and cook once again for another 2 to 3 minutes. Serve.

Nutrition facts:266 calories; 18g fats; 14g carbs;17g protein; 5g fiber; 4g sugar.

Broccoli Noodle with Chickpea and Chicken

Prep time: 15 minutes

Cook time: 20 minutes

Serves: 3

Ingredients:

- ½ tablespoon of EVOO (extra virgin olive oil)

- ¼ teaspoon of oregano flakes

- 2 broccoli stems, spiralized

- 1boneless chicken breast

- ½ cup of canned chickpeas, drained and rinsed

- ½ cup of green peas, cooked

- ½ cup of leeks, sliced thinly

- Pepper and salt, to taste

For the dressing:

- ⅓ cup of feta

- 2 tablespoons of chopped basil

- ½ of chopped shallot

- 1 tablespoon of olive oil

- 1 tablespoon of red wine vinegar

- 1 garlic clove, minced

- 1 tablespoon of lemon juice

- Pepper and salt, to taste

Directions:

1. Season chicken with pepper and salt plus oregano. In a large skillet, heat ½ tablespoon olive oil over medium heat, and add the chicken. Cook the chicken until no longer pink, then set aside.

2. Meanwhile, heat a pot with water and bring to boil. Add the peas with broccoli noodles and cook for around 2 to 3 minutes or until noodles become al dente. Drain, then set aside.

3. Blend all the ingredients for the dressing in a food processor until it becomes creamy. Place all the prepared ingredients in a bowl, then toss well to combine. Serve.

Nutrition facts: 399 calories; 14g fats; 29g carbs; 39g protein; 8g fiber; 5g sugar.

Carrot Noodles and Onion Soup

Prep time: 15 minutes

Cook time: 15 minutes

Serves: 4

Ingredients:

- 2 teaspoons of EVOO (extra virgin olive oil)

- 1 large diced white onion

- 2 celery stalks, diced

- 1 large carrots, peeled and spiralized

- 6 cups of water

- 3 diced scallions

- 8 oz of thinly sliced button mushrooms

- Pepper and salt, to taste

- 2 garlic cloves, minced

Directions:

1. Heat olive oil in a large-sized pan over medium heat, then add onion. Cook for around 5 to 7 minutes or until it becomes soft.

2. Add garlic, water, celery, and pepper and bring to boil. Reduce heat and let simmer for about a minute. Strain the veggies from the broth and replace them with the carrot noodles and mushrooms. Let cook for another 2 to 3 minutes or until the carrots are cooked. Add in the scallions, then simmer for one more minute. Place in bowls, then serve.

Nutrition facts: 46 calories; 3g fats; 5g carbs; 2g protein; 2g fiber; 2g sugar.

Spiralized Veggie with Quinoa

Prep time: 20 minutes

Cook time: 25 minutes

Serves: 2

Ingredients:

- 3 teaspoons of sesame oil

- ⅓ cup of quinoa, dry

- 1 cup of water

- 1 cup of bean sprouts

- ½ large carrot, peeled and spiralized

- 1½ cups of mushrooms of your choice

- 2 cups of spinach

- 2 eggs

- Salt, to taste

- 1 large zucchini, spiralized

- 1 teaspoon of minced garlic

- Sriracha for garnish

Directions:

1. Place the quinoa into a large pot filled with salted water. Cover the pot and bring to a boil over medium-high heat. Once boiled, reduce to a simmer for around 10 to 15 minutes or until it becomes fluffy. Fluff, using a fork, then transfer in a bowl, set aside.

2. Meanwhile, heat 1 teaspoon sesame oil over medium heat and cook carrot noodles for around 2 minutes. Season with salt and continue cooking until it becomes soft. Set aside.

3. Cook the bean sprouts on the same pan, seasoning with salt, for around 2 minutes. Once cooked, set aside.

4. Add another teaspoon of oil, then cook the mushrooms and season with salt. Cook for around 3 to 5 minutes, then set aside.

5. On the same pan once again, add remaining sesame oil and cook spinach with garlic for around 3 minutes or until spinach is wilted, then set aside.

6. Do the same thing with the zucchini noodles, cooking for around 3 to 5 minutes or until cooked according to your preference.

7. Meanwhile, cook eggs according to preference. For example, heat oil in a pan over medium heat, then crack the eggs into the pan. Cook until the tops of the whites are set but the yolk is still runny. Remove the pan from the heat and take the eggs out using a spatula.

8. Assemble all the veggies in bowl. Top it with the cooked egg and drizzle with a bit of sriracha. Serve.

Nutrition facts: 299 calories; 14g fats; 31g carbs; 15g protein; 6g fiber; 9g sugar.

Kale and Spicy Sausage with Spiralized Carrot Noodles

Prep time: 10 minutes

Cook time: 25 minutes

Serves: 4

Ingredients:

- ¾ lb of decased Italian sausage
- ½ cup of onions, diced
- 2 garlic cloves, minced
- 4 cups of chopped kale
- 6 cups of chicken broth
- 1 large carrot, spiralized
- 1 teaspoon of oregano, dried
- 1 teaspoon of red pepper flakes
- ¼ cup of parmesan cheese, shredded
- Pepper and salt, to taste

Directions:

1. Place a large saucepot over medium-high heat.
2. Add in sausage. Crumble and cook for around 10 to 15 minutes or until it becomes brown.
3. Add garlic, onions, pepper and salt. Cook for around 3 minutes or until onions become soft. Add the kale and cook for a minute.

4. Add chicken broth, then oregano and add more heat. Bring to boil. Once boiled, add carrot noodles, then reduce to low heat. Cook for 5 more minutes until the carrots are cooked. Place into bowls, garnish with red pepper flakes and cheese, then serve.

Nutrition facts: 339 calories; 22g fats; 12g carbs; 22g protein; 3g fiber; 4g sugar.

Spiralized Beet Rice with Veggies

Prep time: 15 minutes

Cook time: 15 minutes

Serves: 2

Ingredients:

- 3 small sized beets, spiralized

- 2 minced garlic cloves

- 1 teaspoon of coconut oil

- ½ cup of red bell pepper, diced

- 2 sliced scallions, green and white parts separated

- 2 beaten eggs

- ¼ cup of canned corn kernels, no-salt added, rinsed and drained

- ½ cup of green peas, frozen

- 1 teaspoon of soy sauce

- Salt and pepper, to taste

Directions:

1. Make rice-like beet noodles using food processor, then set aside.

2. Heat oil in a large pan over medium-high heat, then add the bell pepper, garlic and white part of scallions. Cook for around 2 minutes until it becomes soft. Add beet rice and season. Combine well.

3. Create a cavity at the center of the rice mixture, then add the eggs. Scramble in the middle and combine well. Add the corn, soy sauce and peas. Cook for another 2 minutes more, then remove from heat. Transfer to plate and garnish with green scallions on top. Serve.

Nutrition facts: 248 calories; 7g fats; 29g carbs; 12g protein; 9g fiber; 14g sugar.

Kohlrabi Spaghetti with Bacon and Onion

Prep time: 10 minutes

Cook time: 20 minutes

Serves: 4

Ingredients:

- 1 large onion, spiralized

- 5 strips of bacon

- 2 teaspoons of EVOO(extra virgin olive oil), add more for drizzle

- 2 large kohlrabis, peeled and spiralized

- ¼ cup of parmesan cheese, shaved

- Pepper and salt, to taste

Directions:

1. Heat a large pan over medium heat. Add bacon and cook until it becomes crispy, for around 7 to 10 minutes, tossing halfway through. Once cooked, set aside on a paper towels.

2. Remove half of the bacon fat, then add onion. Season with pepper and salt. Cook the onions until caramelized,

for around 10 to 15 minutes. Transfer onions onto a plate and wipe pan clean.

3. Add olive oil and kohlrabi noodles. Season with pepper and salt, then cook for another 5 to 7 minutes or until the kohlrabi wilts. Add in the onions and bacon to combine well.

4. Divide pasta onto plates. Add a drizzle of olive oil and sprinkle parmesan on top, then serve.

Nutrition facts: 139 calories; 9g fats; 24g carbs; 8g protein; 4g fiber; 4g sugar.

Spiralized Butternut Squash with Sage and Brown Butter

Prep time: 10 minutes

Cook time: 10 minutes

Serves: 4

Ingredients:

- 4 cups of butternut squash, spiralized

- 4 tablespoons of butter, unsalted

- 2 teaspoons of EVOO (extra virgin olive oil)

- 10 medium sage leaves

- Pepper and salt, to taste

- Parmesan cheese, grated (optional)

- ¼ cup pomegranate arils, if desired

Directions:

1. Preheat your oven for 400°F.

2. Place the noodles in a line baking pan, then drizzle with EVOO. Toss gently to fully coat the noodles. Bake for around 7 minutes, then remove from oven.

3. Meanwhile, melt the butter in a pan over medium heat, stirring constantly, for around 1 to 2 minutes. Within 1-2 minutes, the butter will begin to brown; add the sage leaves at this time.Stir continuously for around 2 to 3 minutes until it becomes dark and fragrant. Remove from heat, then toss in the squash noodles. Coat well, sprinkle cheese and pomegranate arils on top, if desired. Serve.

Nutrition facts: 220 calories; 14.2g fats; 25.3g carbs; 2.4g protein; 4.7g fiber; 4.6g sugar.

Spiralized Zucchini Soba Noodles

Prep time: 10 minutes

Cook time: 55 minutes

Serves: 2 to 3

Ingredients:

- 1 pack (9.5 ounces) of soba noodles

- 1 zucchini, spiralized

- 2 tablespoons of tamari

- 2 teaspoons of honey

- 1 tablespoon of rice wine vinegar

- 9 ounces of sliced roasted tofu

For the dressing:

- 2 tablespoons of tamari

- 1 tablespoon of rice wine vinegar

- ½ of avocado

- 1 loosely packed cup of rocket

- ½ of lemon, juiced

- 1 garlic clove, minced

- ½ cup of coriander leaves

- ½ tablespoon of honey

- 2 tablespoons sesame oil

- ½ teaspoon minced ginger

- Water

- Sesame seeds, if desired

Directions:

1. Preheat your oven for 395°F.

2. Combine the rice wine vinegar, tamari, and honey with tofu, mix until tofu is completely coated. Marinate for around 20 minutes.

3. Line a baking pan and spray some oil. Add tofu, then bake for about 20 minutes, then flip on the other side. Bake again for another 10 to 15 minutes until golden.

4. Cook the soba noodles according to the packet instructions. Rinse and cool.

5. Meanwhile, combine all dressing ingredients, except coriander leaves and sesame seeds, in the blender and pulse until it becomes smooth. Add water, if it becomes too thick (around 2–3 tablespoons).

6. Combine noodles with dressing, then place in separate bowls. Top with sesame seeds, tofu plus coriander leaves. Serve.

Nutrition facts: 245 calories; 11.9g fats; 27.3g carbs; 8.1g protein; 3.1g fiber; 6g sugar.

Cucumber Noodle Roll-Ups

Prep time: 15 minutes

Cook time: 5 minutes

Serves: 2

Ingredients:

- 4 tablespoons of hummus

- 1 cup of baby spinach leaves

- 1 medium seedless cucumber, spiralized with Blade D (or Blade C), noodles trimmed and patted dry

- 4 slices of deli turkey

- 2 teaspoons of hemp hearts, optional

- Hot sauce for serving

Directions:

1. Lay flat turkey slices and spread about 1 tablespoon of the hummus on each. Top each with hemp hearts.

2. On the far end side, add about ¼ cup of spinach, then top it with cucumber noodles. Roll the turkey slice like a burrito and secure it with a toothpick. Drizzle with hot sauce or you may use as dipping sauce. Serve.

Nutrition facts: 64 calories; 2g fats; 4g carbs; 7g protein; 1g fiber; 1g sugar.

Cod Wrapped with Spiralized Potato

Prep time: 5 minutes

Cook time: 25 minutes

Serves: 2

Ingredients:

- 9 ounces of potatoes, spiralized

- 4 cod fillets, skinless about 5 ounces each

- 3 teaspoons of dill, chopped

- 3 teaspoons of mint, chopped

- 2 teaspoons of black olives, chopped

- ½ dried basil

- 3 teaspoons lemon thyme

- ½ onion, chopped

For salad:

- 1 finely chopped shallot

- 2 sliced medium tomatoes

- 1 tablespoon of olive oil

- 2 tablespoons of chopped parsley

- 1 teaspoon of balsamic vinegar

- Pepper and salt, to taste

Directions:

1. Preheat your oven to 390°F.

2. Cut the cod in the middle to make a top and bottom piece.

3. In a small bowl, combine the onion, herbs and olives, mix well. Add on each fish slice, making sandwich like pieces.

4. Wrap each of the fish with the spiralized potato, season with salt and pepper, then place on a greased baking pan. Bake for around 20 minutes or until the potato is golden.

5. Meanwhile, in a bowl, mix shallot, tomatoes and parsley. Drizzle olive oil and vinegar over the top; gently toss until mixed and season with salt and pepper. Serve with the cod.

Nutrition facts: 391 calories; 8.6g fats; 4.2g sugar.

Potato Salad

Prep time: 10 minutes

Cook time: 10 minutes

Serves: 2

Ingredients:

- 2 large potatoes, peeled and spiralized

- 10 chopped black olives

- ½ jar of roasted red pepper (or cooked fresh red peppers)

- 1 thick slice of roast ham, chopped

- 1 tablespoon of olive oil

- 0.7 ounce of pine nuts

- 10 chopped basil leaves

- Zest of ½ lemon

- Pepper and salt, to taste

Directions:

1. Cook spiralized potatoes in salted boiling water for around 3 to 4 minutes, then drain.

2. Take a dry non-stick pan. Put the pine nuts in it (use no oil) and cook for 2 to 3 minutes over medium heat, stirring frequently or shaking pan until golden. When done, transfer to a large mixing bowl. Add in zest, basil, and olive oil. Add the potatoes, then season with salt and pepper. Toss to combine well.

3. Arrange the roasted red pepper on the plate and the potato salad on top. Sprinkle with olives and ham. Serve.

Nutrition facts: 354 calories; 15.6g fats; 4.5g sugar.

Rainbow Pad Thai Salad

Prep time: 5 minutes

Cook time: 10 minutes

Serves: 2

Ingredients:

- 2 carrots, spiralized

- 1 zucchini, spiralized

- 1 red pepper, sliced thinly

- 1 cup red cabbage, sliced thinly

- ¾ cup of edamame

- 1 teaspoon of sesame seeds

- 1 tablespoon of hemp seeds

- 3 green onions, sliced thinly

For the dressing:

- 1 clove of garlic

- 2 tablespoons of lime juice

- 2 tablespoons of water

- ¼ cup of raw almond butter

- 2 tablespoons of tamari, low sodium

- 2½ teaspoons of maple syrup

- 1 teaspoon of grated ginger

- ½ tablespoon of sesame oil

Directions:

1. Combine all the veggies in a bowl and toss. Set aside.

2. Prepare the dressing by pulsing all the ingredients in a blender until well combined.

3. Add hemp seeds, green onion, edamame and sesame seeds to veggies, then pour dressing. Serve.

Nutrition facts: 420 calories;25.7g fats; 31.1g carbs;19.6g protein;10.4g fiber;15.9g sugar.

Cinnamon and Toasted Coconut Apple Noodles

Prep time: 5 minutes

Cook time: 15 minutes

Serves: 2

Ingredients:

- 1 apple per person, spiralized

- ½ tablespoon of coconut oil

- ⅓ teaspoon of cinnamon

- 1 cup of unsweetened coconut flakes

Directions:

1. Melt the coconut oil in the pan, over medium heat, then add apple noodles. Sauté noodles until softened and warmed through.

2. Add cinnamon. Transform apple noodles to a plate or a bowl.

3. In the same skillet, over medium heat, toss in your unsweetened coconut flakes and allow them to get toasty & brown (keep your eye on them, don't let them burn).Top your apple noodles with the flakes. Serve and enjoy!

Nutrition facts: 241calories; 12g fats; 32g carbs; 5g protein; 4g fiber; 13g sugar.

Sweet Potato Zoodle Ham with Cheese Sandwich

Prep time: 15 minutes

Cook time: 15 minutes

Serves: 2

Ingredients:

- 1 sweet potato, spiralized

- 1 tablespoon of olive oil

- Olive oil cooking spray

- Pepper and salt, to taste

- 1 teaspoon garlic powder

- ½cupdiced ham

- 1 large egg

- ½ cup grated sharp cheddar cheese + 2 tablespoons extra

Directions:

1. Heat a large skillet over medium heat and coat with cooking spray. Add in the sweet potato noodles, garlic powder and season with salt and pepper.

2. Spray the sweet potato noodles with the cooking spray.

3. Cook the noodles for about 5-10 minutes or until they are completely softened.

4. In a separate bowl, combine the noodles with the egg, then add the ham and cheese to the bowl. Mix thoroughly.

5. Heat the same skillet over medium heat, and add in the olive oil. When the oil is hot, drop the noodle mixture into the pan, trying to get it as round as possible.

6. Quickly push together the noodle in the pan with a spatula. Make sure that the sweet potato noodle is spread evenly and there are no holes without noodles. Top with 2 tablespoons of cheese and cook the noodles for about 3 minutes or until the noodles are set on the bottom and have browned.

7. Flip the noodle pancake over carefully and cook on the other side for another 3 minutes or until the noodles have

set and have browned. Push the noodle pancake down to flatten using the spatula. Once done, take it out of the pan and put onto a cutting board to cut the strayed noodle ends. Serve.

Nutrition facts: 286 calories; 6.8g fats; 34g carbs; 21.1g protein;3.5g fiber; 2.8g sugar.

Spiced Pumpkin and Sweet Potato Noodle Waffles

Prep time: 5 minutes

Cook time: 20 minutes

Serves: 2

Ingredients:

- 1 sweet potato, spiralized

- 1 egg, beaten

- 1 teaspoon pumpkin spice

- Maple syrup

- Cooking spray

Directions:

1. Place a large skillet over medium heat and coat with cooking spray.

2. Cook the noodles for about 10 minutes, stirring frequently. Transfer to a bowl and season noodles with pumpkin spice. Mix in the egg.

3. Spray preheated waffle iron with cooking spray. Place the noodles into hot waffle iron. Cook the waffle according to the iron's settings.

4. Serve with maple syrup.

Nutrition facts: 284 calories; 8g fats; 47g carbs;9.7g protein; 7.2g fiber; 6.5g sugar.

Carrot Radish Salad

Prep time: 15 minutes

Serves: 2

Ingredients:

- 7 medium radishes, peeled and spiralized

- 3 cups shredded carrots

- ¼ cup raisins

- Lettuce leaves

For the dressing:

- 2 tablespoons olive oil

- 2 tablespoons lime juice

- ½ teaspoon salt

- ¼ teaspoon pepper

- ½ teaspoon sugar

- ½ teaspoon grated lime peel

Directions:

1. In a bowl, combine the radishes, carrots, and raisins.

2. In a small mixing bowl, whisk the olive oil, lime juice, salt, pepper, sugar, and lime peel. Mix until smooth. Pour the prepared dressing over the salad. Toss together until everything is well coated. Serve in a bowl lined with lettuce leaves if desired.

Nutrition facts: 77 calories; 0g fats; 18g carbs; 3g protein; 5g fiber; 8g sugar.

Butternut Squash Fettucine with Sausage Ragu

Prep time: 20 minutes

Cook time: 60 minutes

Serves: 4

Ingredients:

- 1 diced sweet onion

- 2 garlic cloves, minced

- 12 oz of Italian sausage, spicy, crumbled and decased

- ¼ teaspoon of red pepper flakes

- 1½ tablespoons of tomato paste

- ¼ cup of red wine

- 28 oz (1 can) of peeled plum tomatoes

- 1 teaspoon basil, dried

- 1 teaspoon oregano, dried

- 4 cups of Tuscan kale, chopped

- 1 cup canned white beans, rinsed and drained

- 1 bay leaf

- 2 butternut squash, spiralized

- Basil, to garnish

- Pepper and salt, to taste

- Parmesan cheese, grated

- Olive oil

Directions:

1. Preheat your oven to 400°F.

2. Heat a large pot, over medium heat, add sausage and crumble further. Cook for around 10 minutes or until it becomes brown. Add in garlic, onions, red pepper flakes, then cook for another 2 to 3 minutes.

3. Crush the tomatoes to the pot using your hands. Add tomato paste, basil, bay leaf, wine, and oregano. Season with salt and pepper. Increase heat and bring to boil. Once boiling, reduce the heat and simmer for around 30 to 35 minutes. Add beans and kale, then cook for 5 minutes more or until sauce becomes thick like ragu. Remove the bay leaf.

4. Meanwhile, place the butternut noodles on a lined baking pan. Drizzle with olive oil and massage them thoroughly. Season with salt and pepper and roast in the oven for around 8 to 10 minutes or until it becomes al dente.

5. Transfer butternut squash to bowls, then top with the ragu. Top with cheese and fresh basil. Serve.

Nutrition facts: 577 calories; 28g fats; 52g carbs; 27g protein; 12g fiber; 15g sugar.

Red Cabbage with Crusted Tuna

Prep time: 25 minutes

Cook time: 5 minutes

Serves: 3

Ingredients:

- 1 tablespoon of sesame seeds, white

- 1 tablespoon of sesame seeds, black

- 1 red cabbage, spiralized

- ¼ cup of scallions, chopped

- ½ tablespoon of EVOO(extra virgin olive oil)

- 1 ahi tuna steak, around 8 ounces

For the dressing:

- 1½ teaspoons of honey

- 1½ teaspoons of soy sauce

- 1½ tablespoons of rice wine vinegar

- 1 tablespoon of sesame oil

- 2 tablespoons of tahini

- Pepper and salt, to taste

Directions:

1. Put all dressing ingredients in a blender and process until it becomes creamy.

2. Place cabbage and scallions in a bowl, then add dressing. Toss and set aside.

3. Heat olive oil in a large skillet, over medium heat.

4. Mix black and white sesame seeds. Press each side of the tuna in the mixture and cook tuna in a heated pan for around 1 to2 minutes, then flip and cook for another minute. Once done, remove from heat, then thinly slice. Place on top of the cabbage salad. Serve.

Nutrition facts: 299 calories; 17g fats; 17g carbs; 21g protein; 7g fiber; 8g sugar.

Sweet Potato Fries with Lime and Chipotle Aioli

Prep time: 5 minutes

Cook time: 40 minutes

Serves: 4

Ingredients:

- 2 sweet potatoes, spiralized
- Olive oil cooking spray
- Pepper and salt, to taste

Aioli:

- ½ lime, juiced
- ½ chipotle in adobo pepper
- 1 cup of Greek yogurt
- Pepper and salt, to taste

Directions:

1. Preheat your oven to 400°F.

2. Add the sweet potatoes on a lined baking tray. Spray the tray with the olive oil, then season with pepper and salt. Bake for around 35 to 40 minutes or until fries become crispy.

3. Meanwhile, place the Greek yogurt, salt and pepper, lime juice, and chipotle in blender and process on low speed until well blended. Adjust the taste, according to preference. Serve with the fries.

Nutrition facts: 100 calories; 0g fats; 17g carbs; 7g protein; 2g fiber; 6g sugar.

Cabbage Jicama Salad with Mango and Almond Dressing

Prep time: 30 minutes

Serves: 4

Ingredients:

- 1 medium jicama, peeled and spiralized

- 1 cup of edamame, cooked

- 1 cup scallions, diced

- 1 cup of red cabbage, spiralized

- 1 avocado, if desired

For the dressing:

- 1 tablespoon of rice vinegar

- ¼ cup almond milk, unsweetened

- 1½ cups of diced mango

- 1½ tablespoons of cilantro, chopped

- ¼ teaspoon of red pepper flakes

- 2 tablespoons of lime juice

- Salt, to taste

Directions:

1. Put all dressing ingredients in a blender. Puree until smooth. Adjust taste, if needed.

2. Combine the jicama, scallions, edamame, and cabbage in a bowl and add dressing. Toss to combine. Chill for around 10 minutes, then serve. You can garnish them with sliced avocado, if desired.

Nutrition facts: 124 calories; 3g fats; 19g carbs; 8g protein; 6g fiber; 7g sugar.

Spiralized Zucchini Noodles with Chicken and Peanut Sauce

Prep time: 5 minutes

Cook time: 15 minutes

Serves: 4

Ingredients:

- 1 lb of diced chicken tenders

- 4 tablespoons of grape seed oil

- 2 zucchini, spiralized

- 1 carrot, spiralized

- ⅓ cup bean sprouts

- ¼ cup diced fresh cilantro

- ¼ cup diced green onions

- 1 julienned red pepper

- Sesame seeds, for garnish

Peanut sauce:

- 4 tablespoons peanut butter

- 1 minced garlic clove

- Juice of 1 lime

- 3 tablespoons coconut aminos

- ¼ teaspoon red pepper flakes

- ½ teaspoon ginger, ground

Directions:

1. Place the peanut butter, garlic, coconut aminos, lime juice, ginger, and red pepper flakes in a bowl and mix well to combine. Set aside.

2. Heat 2 tablespoons of grape seed oil in a large skillet over medium high heat. Add chicken tenders. Cook for 8 minutes, flipping halfway through cooking. Dice when cooled.

3. Using the same pan, add the rest of the grape seed oil, then add carrot and zucchini noodles. Stir fry for around 2 minutes. Remove noodles and put them in a large bowl. Add the chicken, bean sprouts, cilantro, red pepper, green onions and peanut sauce. Toss to combine and serve. Garnish with sesame seeds.

Nutrition facts: 363 calories; 18g carbs; 31g protein; 6g fiber; 7g sugar.

Spiralized Apple Strings with Chocolate

Prep time: 5 minutes

Cook time: 3 hours to freeze

Serves: 3

Ingredients:

- 3 apples, spiralized

- 10 oz of mini-choco chips

- Toppings, to taste

Directions:

1. Line a large baking tray with parchment paper. Place the apples onto baking tray.

2. Melt the chocolate. Place the chocolate into a heatproof bowl. Then place bowl over a pan of barely simmering water and allow the chocolate to melt, stirring occasionally, until it becomes smooth.

3. Drizzle the chocolate on the apples and top with preferred topping. Freeze for about 3 hours but preferably overnight. Serve frozen.

Nutrition facts: 153 calories; 8g fats; 21g carbs; 2g protein; 3g fiber; 16g sugar.

Two Cheese Zoodles

Prep Time: 5 minutes

Cook Time: 20 minutes

Total Time: 25 minutes

Serves: 4

Ingredients:

- 6 zucchinis

- ⅓ cup finely grated Pecorino

- ¾ cup finely grated Grana Padano or Parmesan cheese, plus ¼ cup, for garnish

- 1 tablespoon ground black pepper, plus more for finishing the dish

- 2 tablespoons olive oil

Directions:

1. Using a spiralizer, create zucchini "noodles".

2. Heat olive oil in a large pan over medium-high heat. Once oil heats, add in the noodles and cook for about 2 to 3 minutes, until zucchini are tender but still retain some crunch.

3. Let the noodles rest for about 3 minutes so that they can release all the moisture.

4. Transfer noodles to a bowl and reserve the excess water in a small bowl. In another large bowl, combine the cheeses and black pepper; add just enough zoodle water to make a thick paste.

5. Add noodles, stir and toss until everything is evenly coated in sauce ingredients.

6. Add some olive oil and a bit of zoodle water to thin the sauce if necessary.

7. Sprinkle with additional grated cheese and pepper. Serve immediately.

Nutrition Facts

Per serving | Calories: 247 | Fat: 17g | Carbohydrates: 6g | Protein: 9g |

Parmesan Chicken Zoodles & Sun Dried Tomato Sauce

Prep Time: 15 minutes

Cook Time: 25 minutes

Total Time: 40 minutes

Serves: 6

Ingredients:

- 1½ lbs skinless chicken thigh fillets, cut into strips
- 1 tablespoon butter
- 3.5 oz jar sun dried tomatoes in oil, chopped
- 4 oz fresh semi-dried tomato strips in oil, chopped*
- 4 cloves garlic, peeled and crushed
- 1¼ cup thickened cream, reduced fat or full fat (or half and half)
- 1 cup shaved Parmesan cheese

- 2 large zucchini (or summer squash)
- Dried basil seasoning
- Red chilli flakes
- Salt to taste

Directions:

1. In a large skillet over medium high heat, melt the butter. Add the chicken strips and sprinkle with salt. Pan fry until the chicken is cooked through and golden brown on the outside.

2. Add both semi-dried and sun dried tomatoes with 1 tablespoon of the oil from the jar (optional but adds extra flavour), and add the garlic; sauté until fragrant.

3. Meanwhile, use a spiralizer to turn the zucchini into "noodles". Set aside.

4. Lower heat, add the Parmesan cheese and the cream; simmer while stirring until the cheese has melted through. Sprinkle over salt, basil and red chilli flakes to your taste.

5. Add in the zucchini and toss until well coated. Continue to simmer until the zoodles have softened to your liking (about 5-8 minutes).

6. Serve.

*If you can't find semi-dried tomato strips, substitute with an extra jar of sun-dried tomatoes

Nutrition Facts

Per serving | Calories: 394 | Fat: 22.6g | Carbohydrates: 9.2g | Protein: 35.6g | Fiber: 0.8g

Zoodles with Creamy Garlic Cashew Sauce

Prep Time: about 8 hours (for soaking)

Cook Time: 20 minutes

Serves: 4

Ingredients:

- 6 medium-large zucchini

- 2 tablespoons olive oil

- 1 cup cashews

- 1 tablespoon lemon juice

- ¾ cup water (more for soaking)

- 1 clove garlic

- ½ teaspoon fine grain salt

- ½ teaspoon ground black pepper

Note: This recipe makes more than enough sauce — enough for at least 6 or 8 servings, if not more. Don't worry you'll be able to find ways to use the leftover sauce, it will also keep in the fridge for a few days, and it can be frozen too.

Directions:

1. Place cashews in a bowl and cover with water. Let soak for at least 8 hours or overnight. Rinse and drain. Add the cashews, salt, garlic, lemon juice and ¾ cup fresh filtered water to the blender or food processor and blend until smooth. Take a taste and adjust seasoning as needed.

2. Using a spiralizer, make the zucchini noodles.

3. Heat 1 tablespoon of olive oil in a skillet set over medium-high heat. Once hot, add zoodles and cook until just tender, yet still crisp, about 2 to 3 minutes.

4. Let the noodles rest for about 3 minutes so that they can release all the moisture. Transfer noodles to a colander and drain the excess water from the pan.

5. Wipe the pan and heat the remaining tablespoon of olive oil over medium-high heat. Add about ½ of the cashew sauce and zoodles, stir vigorously to coat them with the sauce. Sauté for 2 minutes, stirring constantly until heated through.

6. Season with salt and pepper to taste and serve.

Nutrition Facts

Per serving | Calories: 125 | Fat: 7g | Carbohydrates: 12g | Protein: 5g |

Quinoa and Cucumber Noodles Salad with Mango

Prep Time: 10 minutes

Cook Time: 5 minutes

Total Time: 15 minutes

Serves: 2

Ingredients:

- 1 large cucumber

- ¼ cup to ⅓ cup cooked quinoa*

- ⅓ cup mango, peeled and cubed

- 2 -3 tablespoons dried cranberries

- 2 -3 tablespoons pumpkin seed

- 1-2 fresh basil leaves

- 2 teaspoons balsamic glaze

- 1-2 teaspoons avocado oil or olive oil

- ½ teaspoon grated fresh ginger

- Fresh ground pepper (to taste)

- Sea salt (to taste)

Directions:

1. Wash all your fruit/vegetables. Spiralize your cucumber and place in a large bowl.

2. Add the mango and quinoa. Add the rest of the ingredients; toss well.

3. Serve immediately or place in fridge for later.

*Notes: Make sure your quinoa is cooked and fluffed, not soggy. Feel free to use another gluten free grain like cooked rice, millet, buckwheat.

Nutrition Facts

Per serving | Calories: 334 | Fat: 16.5g | Carbohydrates: 43.3g | Sugars: 22.8g | Protein: 9.4g|

Stir Fry Casserole

Prep Time: 10 minutes

Cook Time: 40 minutes

Total Time: 50 minutes

Serves: 5

Ingredients:

1 lb boneless chicken thighs or breast (the darker meat works best)

For Stir Fry Sauce:

- 2 tablespoons fish sauce

- 2 tablespoons chili garlic sauce/paste (you can use Sriracha as substitute)

- 2-3 tablespoons gluten free Tamari soy sauce mixed with 1 tablespoon dark sugar (coconut palm sugar, dark brown sugar, or molasses). This creates a dark soy sauce.

- ¼ teaspoon lime zest (a splash of juice works too)

- Pinch of ground ginger

- Salt and pepper (to taste)

Other Ingredients:

- 2 large zucchini

- 1 cup chopped onion

- 1 teaspoon minced garlic

- 1 tablespoon olive oil or sesame oil

- 1 cup stir fry veggies (i.e. broccoli, snap peas, etc.)

- 2-3 tablespoons tapioca starch or potato starch/flour

- 1 red bell pepper, sliced

- 2-3 tablespoons coconut milk

- 3 eggs

For garnish:

- Thai basil

- Optional finely diced Thai bird's eye red pepper for extra spicy*

- Optional sesame seeds to garnish

Directions:

1. Clean your chicken, then cut your chicken meat into small cubes. Set aside.

2. Slice veggies and create zucchini noodles using spiralizer. Pat the zucchini noodles dry with paper towels to absorb any excess moisture.

3. In a large mixing bowl, whisk all the ingredients for the stir-fry sauce.

4. Preheat oven to 350°F and grease casserole dish (8" x 11"). Set aside.

5. Place the garlic, onion, chicken and oil in a skillet or large pan. Sauté 5 minutes.

6. Add your stir fry veggies, sauce, sliced red bell pepper and 2-3 tablespoons tapioca starch. Stir fry 10-15 minutes until chicken is no longer pink (but not overcooked) and starch is mixed well with the meat and veggies.

7. Place zucchini noodles at the bottom of your casserole dish.

8. Add the chicken and veggies, stir fry with sauce on top of zucchini noodles; toss evenly.

9. Whisk eggs and coconut milk together in a small bowl. Pour over casserole dish.

10. Bake until the edges are golden brown and the egg mix is cooked through, about 25-30 minutes.

11. Remove from oven and garnish with Thai basil and optional sliced Thai peppers.

12. Adjust salt and pepper to taste. Sprinkle with sesame seeds over top, if desired.

13. Serve.

*Notes: You can use any other spicy red pepper as a substitute.

Nutrition Facts

Per serving | Calories: 264 | Fat: 13.7 g | Carbohydrates: 12.1g | Sugars: 6.2g | Protein: 23.1g |

Zucchini Pasta with Meatballs

Prep Time: 15 minutes

Cook Time: 40-45 minutes

Total Time: about 1 hour

Serves: 6

Ingredients:

For the meatballs:

- 1½ pounds 93% lean ground turkey meat

- 1½ cups fresh whole-wheat breadcrumbs

- 3 tablespoons milk

- 1 large egg yolk

- ½ cup grated Parmesan

- ¼ cup parsley leaves, minced

- 2 cloves garlic, finely minced

- 1 tablespoon olive oil

- ¾ teaspoon salt

- ¼ teaspoon ground black pepper

For the noodles:

- 6 large zucchini squash (6 ounces each), washed and peeled

- 2 teaspoons sea salt

For the sauce:

- 3 (14.5-ounces) cans diced tomatoes

- 1 medium onion, chopped

- 4 garlic cloves, minced

- 1 teaspoon olive oil

- ¼ teaspoon red pepper flakes

Directions:

1. *For the meatballs*: In a large bowl, mix the breadcrumbs together with the milk, and egg yolk. Allow the milk to soak into the breadcrumbs for at least 5 minutes. Once the milk has absorbed some of the breadcrumbs, add in the turkey, parsley, Parmesan, garlic, salt and pepper. Mix well with your hands to combine.

Roll the meatball mixture into 18 one-inch meatballs. Put them on a plate, then cover with clingfilm and stick them in the freezer for 20 minutes. In the meantime, make the noodles and tomato sauce.

2. *For the zucchini noodles*: Preheat oven to 200°F and line a rimmed baking sheet with 2-3 layers of paper towels. Cut the zucchini into noodles with a spiralizer. Arrange the noodles on the baking sheet and sprinkle with salt. Bake for 30 minutes.

3. *For the tomato sauce*: Place 2 cans of tomato sauce in a food processor and blend until smooth. In large saucepan, heat 1 teaspoon of oil over medium-low heat until hot. Add the onion and cook until soft, about 8 minutes. Stir in the garlic and red pepper flakes and cook for 30 seconds. Add the tomato puree and remaining can of diced tomatoes; simmer for 10 minutes.

4. Heat 1 tablespoon of the oil in a large nonstick skillet over medium heat. Add the meatballs in a single layer to the hot oil and fry for about 8 to10 minutes, turning frequently, until browned all over.

5. Transfer the meatballs to the tomato sauce to finish cooking, about 10 minutes.

6. When the noodles are done, gently squeeze them in the paper towel to wring out any additional water.

7. Divide the noodles into 6 bowls and top each with 3 meatballs and sauce, or alternatively, toss the noodles

into the sauce and simmer for 5 minutes for softer noodles.

Nutrition Facts

Per serving | Calories: 440 | Fat: 16 g | Carbohydrates: 42.7g | Sugars: 13.9g | Fiber: 8g | Protein: 35.8g |

Buffalo Cauliflower with Sweet Potato Noodles

Prep Time: 20 minutes + about 2 hours (for soaking)

Cook Time: 30 minutes

Serves: 4

Ingredients:

- 1 medium head of cauliflower, chopped into florets (about 8 cups)
- Salt and pepper (to taste)
- 2 tablespoons olive oil
- 3 tablespoons coconut oil
- ¼ cup raw cashews, soaked in water for at least 2 hours
- Vegetable broth, if needed
- 2 large sweet potatoes, peeled, Blade B, noodles trimmed

- 1 tablespoon chopped parsley, to garnish

For the buffalo pasta sauce:

- 3-4 tablespoons hot sauce (I use Tessemae's)
- 1 tablespoon freshly squeezed lemon juice
- 1 teaspoon paprika
- 1 teaspoon garlic powder
- 1 tablespoon apple cider vinegar

- Salt (to taste)

Directions:

1. Preheat the oven to 400°F. Place the cauliflower florets in a large bowl, drizzle with 1 tablespoon of olive oil and sprinkle with the salt, toss to combine. Transfer the seasoned cauliflower florets on a baking sheet and spread into an even layer. Roast for 20-25 minutes, stirring once or twice, until the cauliflower is tender and golden brown.
2. On another baking sheet, lay the potato noodles in 1 layer. Drizzle with 1 tablespoon of olive oil and sprinkle with salt and pepper. Roast for 17-20 minutes or until cooked through, but still al dente (taste test.)
3. While the cauliflower and sweet potato roasts, puree the cashews in a high-speed blender or food processor until creamy. Set aside.
4. Melt coconut oil in a medium pot over medium heat, until it becomes liquid. Add the coconut oil to the cashew cream along with the other ingredients for the buffalo sauce and puree again until creamy. If needed, add in vegetable broth until it reaches a sauce-like consistency

(not runny, but not too thick) Cover and set aside, to keep warm.

5. In a large mixing bowl, toss together the cauliflower florets with half of the buffalo sauce mixture, keeping the remaining sauce in the pot. Spread evenly onto baking sheet. Place back in the oven and bake for 5 more minutes or until sauce begins to bubble.

6. Place the sweet potatoes onto a plate and top with cauliflower florets. Pour the remaining sauce over the top. Serve immediately, garnished with parsley.

Nutrition Facts

Per serving | Calories: 254 | Fat: 12 g | Carbohydrates: 33g | Sugars: 13g | Protein: 6g |

Sweet Potato Coconut Curry Recipe

Prep Time: 5 minutes

Cook Time: 25 minutes

Serves: 2

Ingredients:

For the Curry:

- ½ tablespoon coconut oil

- 1 cup broccoli, cut into bite-sized pieces

- 1 large carrot, peeled and sliced, about a heaping ½ cup

- 1 small red bell pepper, sliced, about 1 cup

- ⅓ cup onion, chopped, about half a small onion

- 1 teaspoon fresh ginger, minced

- 1 (13.5 ounces) can full fat coconut milk

- ½ tablespoon yellow curry powder

- Pinch of salt

For the Sweet Potato Noodles:

- ½ tablespoon coconut oil

- 1 large sweet potato, peeled,

- Pinch of salt

For the Mango Salsa:

- 1 mango, large, diced, about ¾ cup

- 2 tablespoons red onion, diced

- ½ teaspoon apple cider vinegar

- ¼ cup fresh cilantro, plus additional for garnish

- 1 red chili, Thai, minced, adjust to preferred level of spiciness

- Pinch of salt

Directions:

1. Heat a large saucepan or pot to medium- high heat, add ½ tablespoon coconut oil and cook the carrots for about 3 minutes, until they just begin to soften.

2. Turn the heat down to medium and add the onion, ginger, broccoli, pepper and stir. Cook, stirring frequently, until softened, about 5 minutes.

3. Add in the ½ tablespoon of yellow curry powder and cook until fragrant, about 1 minute.

4. Add in the can of coconut milk (make sure you mix it well before adding!) and a pinch of salt, mixing well.

5. Bring to a boil over medium-high heat. Once boiling, reduce the heat to low and simmer, stirring occasionally, until the sauce begins to thicken, about 15 minutes.

6. While the sauce cooks, cut the sweet potatoes into noodles with a spiralizer, using the ⅛-inch blade (3 mm, blade C).

7. Heat the remaining coconut oil in a separate pan over medium heat. Then add spiralized sweet potatoes to the

pan and cook covered, stirring often, for 8-10 minutes or until softened. Season with salt.

8. While you wait, toss together the diced mango, red onion, apple cider vinegar, Thai chili and cilantro in a medium bowl. Season with a pinch of salt.

9. Divide the sweet potato noodles between two plates and top with the curry. Garnish with the mango salsa and extra cilantro.

Nutrition Facts

Per serving | Calories: 563 | Fat: 39.9 g | Carbohydrates: 51.8g | Sugars: 19.3g | Protein: 8.3g |

Parmesan Potato Noodles

Prep Time: 10 minutes

Cook Time: 20 minutes

Serves: 6

Ingredients:

- 2 pounds red potatoes, Blade C, noodles trimmed

- 1 tablespoon extra virgin olive oil

- ½ teaspoon garlic powder

- Salt and pepper, to taste

- 1½ tablespoons freshly grated parmesan cheese

- 2 tablespoons minced parsley, to garnish

Directions:

1. Preheat oven to 425°F.

2. Toss the potato noodles in a bowl with olive oil, garlic powder, salt and pepper.

3. Arrange noodles onto a parchment-paper lined baking sheet and bake for 12-15 minutes, until they start to turn golden brown.

4. Remove the potato noodles from the oven and set it to broil. Sprinkle the potatoes with parmesan cheese and put back in the oven for 3-5 minutes or until golden brown, careful not to burn (a few burnt edges are okay.)

5. Remove from the oven, sprinkle with minced parsley and transfer to a serving bowl.

Nutrition Facts

Per serving | Calories: 162 | Fat: 3 g | Carbohydrates: 30g | Sugars: 2g | Protein: 4g |

Honey Garlic Shrimp with Spiralized Squash & Zucchini

Prep Time: 5 minutes

Cook Time: 15 minutes

Serves: 4

Ingredients:

- ½ cup chicken broth

- 3 tablespoons French's Sweet or Spicy Yellow Mustard

- ¼ cup honey

- 1 tablespoon lemon juice

- 2 yellow squash

- 2 zucchini

- 2 tablespoons olive oil

- 2 red bell pepper, cut into ¼-inch dice

- 3-4 cloves garlic, minced

- ¼ teaspoon red pepper flakes

- 1½ pounds shrimp, peeled, deveined, tails removed

- Salt and freshly ground black pepper (to taste)

- Chopped parsley, for garnish

Directions:

1. Combine broth, French's Sweet or Spicy Yellow Mustard, honey, and lemon juice. Set aside.

2. Spiralize the zucchini and squash into thin strips, using spiralizer.

3. In a large skillet, heat the olive oil over medium-high heat. Add diced red bell pepper. Sauté the peppers, stirring and turning frequently, until edges just start to brown.

4. Add garlic and red pepper flakes and stir until fragrant and combined, about 30 seconds.

5. Add shrimp. Sprinkle with salt and freshly ground black pepper to taste. Cook for 1 minute.

6. Add honey mustard mixture, zucchini, and squash. Cook for 2-3 minutes, until veggies have cooked down and shrimp is opaque. Garnish with a sprinkle of chopped parsley and serve.

Nutrition Facts

Per serving | Calories: 382 | Fat: 10.5 g | Carbohydrates: 31.2g | Sugars: 23.3g | Protein: 42g |

Spiralized Apple and Parmesan Salad

Prep Time: 5 minutes

Cook Time: 10 minutes

Serves: 4

Ingredients:

Salad

- 4 medium apples (try a sweet and crisp variety like Pink Lady or Honey Crisp)

- ½ cup shredded Parmesan cheese

- ¼ cup finely chopped chives

Dressing

- Juice of 1 lemon

- 1 teaspoon Dijon mustard

- ½ clove garlic

- 1 tablespoon olive oil

- Dash of salt and pepper

Directions:

1. In a bowl, whisk the dressing ingredients together until combined well. Set aside.

2. Spiralize apple, using the smallest blade, leaving the peel on. Discard core and seeds. Add the apples, parmesan cheese, and chives to a large bowl and toss together.

3. Pour dressing over apple mixture; toss gently to coat.

Nutrition Facts

Per serving | Calories: 171 | Fat: 5.9 g | Carbohydrates: 26.8g | Sugars: 19.4g | Protein: 4.8g |

Chipotle Sweet Potato Noodle Salad with Roasted Corn

Prep Time: 10 minutes

Cook Time: 15 minutes

Serves: 4

Ingredients:

For the sweet potato noodles salad:

- 2 sweet potatoes, spiralized

- 4 ears sweet corn (kernels cut off the cob)

- 1 cup chopped fresh cilantro

- 1 cup chopped fresh spinach

- ½ cup pepitas

- Olive oil

For the chipotle dressing:

- ⅓ cup olive oil

- 3 tablespoons water

- 2 individual chipotle peppers, canned in adobo sauce

- 1 teaspoon agave or honey

- 1 clove garlic

- Juice of one lemon or lime

- Juice of one orange

- Generous pinch of salt

Directions:

1. For the sweet potato noodles salad: in a large cast-iron (or stainless steel) skillet, heat the olive oil over medium heat. Add the sweet potato noodles then cook, tossing gently with tongs, until softened, about 2-3 minutes.

2. Wipe the skillet out so it's dry. Add the corn to the skillet and turn the heat to medium high.*

3. Cook until it is browned and cooked through, about 4 to 5 minutes. Stir the corn once or twice during cooking, allowing it to remain undisturbed for most of the cooking time.

4. Combine the corn, cilantro, spinach, pepitas and noodles together in a bowl.

5. For the chipotle dressing:blend the dressing ingredients in a blender or food processor until smooth. Taste and adjust to your liking.

6. Pour dressing over salad and toss.

*Note: The idea is to dry roast the corn without oil or butter. They don't get as browned and roasty if you have to put butter or oil in the pan. So, make sure you're using a high quality pan - cast iron skillets are best, but stainless steel skillets will work fine as well.

Nutrition Facts

Per serving | Calories: 369 | Fat: 26.3 g | Carbohydrates: 30.1g | Sugars: 7.7g | Protein: 8.3g |

Thai Peanut Zucchini Noodles

Prep Time: 10 minutes

Cook Time: 5 minutes

Serves: 4

Ingredients:

- 4 small zucchinis, spiralized

- 1 carrot, spiralized

- ½ red bell pepper, cut into match sticks

- 1 tablespoon coconut oil

- ¼ cup fresh cilantro

- 3 scallions, chopped

- ¼ cup peanuts, chopped

- 4 lime slices

For the Peanut Sauce:

- ¼ cup smooth all-natural peanut butter

- 2 tablespoons fresh lime juice

- 1 garlic clove, minced

- 3 tablespoons Bragg's Amino Acids (or soy sauce or tamari)

- 2 tablespoons toasted sesame seed oil

- ½ teaspoon ground ginger

- ¼ teaspoon crushed red pepper flakes (or to taste)

- Water for thinning as needed (about 1-2 tablespoons)

Directions:

1. Combine all ingredients of the peanut sauce in a bowl. Mix with a whisk until well blended. Set aside.

2. Heat the coconut oil in a large skillet over medium high heat. When the oil is hot, add the zucchini, peppers, carrot and sauté for 1-2 minutes, until tender but still slightly crisp (but not mushy).

3. Remove from heat and stir in sauce.

4. Sprinkle with the cilantro, scallions and peanuts.

5. Serve with a slice of lime and enjoy.

Nutrition Facts

Per serving | Calories: 251 | Fat: 22 g | Carbohydrates: 9g | Sugars: 4g | Protein: 7g |

Zucchini Noodles with Creamy Avocado Pesto

Prep Time: 5 minutes

Cook Time: 5-7 minutes

Serves: 8

Ingredients:

- 6 large zucchini, spiralized

- 1 tablespoon olive oil

- Parmesan cheese (to taste)

- Cracked black pepper (to taste)

For the Sauce:

- 2 ripe avocados

- 3 cloves garlic

- 1 cup fresh basil leaves

- ¼ cup pine nuts

- 2 tablespoons lemon juice

- 3 tablespoons olive oil

- ½ teaspoon sea salt

Directions:

1. Make zucchini noodles by using a spiralizer. Set aside on paper towels to soak up any excess water.

2. To make the dressing, place the avocado, garlic, pine nuts, basil leaves, lemon juice and sea salt in a food processor and pulse until finely chopped. Then, with the motor still running, add olive oil in a slow stream until emulsified and creamy.

3. Heat the olive oil in a large skillet over medium-high heat. Add the zucchini noodles and stir-fry until just cooked but still crunchy, about 2 minutes. Season with cracked pepper.

4. Remove from heat and serve immediately, sprinkled with grated Parmesan.

Nutrition Facts

Per serving | Calories: 214 | Fat: 17.1 g | Carbohydrates: 13.2g | Sugars: 4.2g | Protein: 4.8g |

Butternut Squash & Sage Spaghetti with Zucchini Noodles

Prep Time: 10 minutes

Cook Time: 35-40 minutes

Serves: 4

Ingredients:

- 2 tablespoons olive oil

- 3 cloves garlic, minced

- 1 medium onion, chopped into large chunks

- 2 lbs butternut squash, peeled and cut into cubes (about 3 cups)

- ¼ teaspoon nutmeg

- Salt and pepper (to taste)

- 3 sage leaves, minced

- 8 oz Barilla whole wheat spaghetti

- 2 cups vegetable broth

- 2 medium zucchini, spiralized

Directions:

1. In a large skillet over medium heat, warm the olive oil. Add the garlic and onion and cook, stirring constantly, until just golden and fragrant, about 2 to 3 minutes.

2. Add squash, nutmeg, salt and pepper, cover and cook, stirring occasionally, for about 8 minutes. Add sage and cook for one more minute.

3. Add vegetable broth and bring to a boil. Reduce heat and allow squash to simmer, uncovered, for about 20 minutes until the squash is soft and the broth is reduced by half.

4. Meanwhile, set your pasta pot on the stove and bring salted water to a boil. Cook according to package instructions (usually 10 to 12 minutes).

5. Drain the pasta in a colander. Rinse with cool water to prevent sticking and set aside.

6. Once the squash mixture is ready and has cooled slightly, place mixture into food processor and process until smooth. Feel free to add extra vegetable broth or water as-needed for a thinner sauce.

7. Toss the zucchini noodles, spaghetti and sauce all together in the skillet you were just using and cook over medium heat for about 2 minutes, until everything is combined. Season with additional salt and pepper and sage.

8. Serve and enjoy!

Nutrition Facts

Per serving | Calories: 322 | Fat: 8 g | Carbohydrates: 54g | Sugars: 8.7g | Protein: 10.6g |

Zucchini Noodle Caprese with Chicken

Prep Time: 10 minutes

Cook Time: 20 minutes

Serves: 4

Ingredients:

- 3 boneless, skinless chicken breasts, cut into ½-inch cubes

- ½ teaspoon dried Italian seasoning

- 2 large zucchini, spiralized

- 3 garlic cloves, minced

- 1cup halved grape tomatoes

- 1 tablespoon chopped fresh basil

- 2 oz fresh mini mozzarella balls, cut in half

- 2 tablespoons balsamic vinegar

- Sea salt and fresh ground pepper (to taste)

- 1½ tablespoons olive oil (or coconut oil)

Directions:

1. Make zucchini noodles by using a spiralizer.

2. Preheat olive oil (or coconut oil) in a skillet over medium-high heat.

3. Place the chicken in the skillet, season with Italian seasoning. Do not add any liquid and do not cover the skillet. Cook until chicken is no longer pink and cooked

through, about 5-8 minutes. As the chicken cooks, turn it occasionally so it browns evenly.

4. Remove chicken from skillet and set aside.

5. Add the garlic and tomatoes to the skillet and cook on medium-low until tomatoes are soft, about 10 minutes.

6. Return heat to medium-high and add back the chicken. Add the balsamic vinegar, zucchini noodles and basil. Stir to get everything well mixed and heat for 2 minutes. Remove skillet from heat and add mozzarella. Serve immediately.

Nutrition Facts

Per serving | Calories: 202 | Fat: 2.7 g | Carbohydrates: 8.9g | Fiber: 2.1g |

Pesto Cucumber Noodles with Honey Chicken and Blueberry Salsa

Prep Time: 10 minutes, plus 2 hours (marinating time)

Cook Time: 25 minutes

Serves: 2

Ingredients:

For the chicken:

- 8 oz Chicken breast

- 2 tablespoons Fresh lime juice

- 2 teaspoon Jalapeno Tabasco sauce

- 2½ teaspoons Honey

- Salt and pepper

For the salsa:

- ¾ cup fresh blueberries, halved

- 2 tablespoons jalapeno, minced (seeds removed)

- 4 teaspoons red onion, minced

- 1 tablespoon fresh basil, thinly sliced

- 2 teaspoons fresh lime juice

For the pesto:

- ¼ cup avocado, mashed (one small avocado)

- 1 teaspoon fresh garlic, minced

- Squeeze of fresh lime juice

- 1 tablespoon extra virgin olive oil

- 1 cup fresh basil, tightly packed

- ¼ teaspoon salt

- Pinch of pepper

- 1 large cucumber, spiralized with Blade B

Directions:

1. In a medium bowl, whisk together the lime juice, Tabasco sauce, honey and a pinch of salt and pepper. Add the chicken and toss to coat with marinade. Cover bowl with plastic wrap and let the chicken marinade for at least 2 hours in the refrigerator.

2. Once marinated, heat your oven to 350°F. Place the chicken breasts in a single layer in a baking dish. Bake until the chicken is cooked through and no longer pink, about 25-30 minutes.

3. Combine all the salsa ingredients in a small bowl and season with a pinch of salt and pepper. Set aside.

4. To make the pesto, combine garlic, avocado and a squeeze of lime juice in the bowl of a food processor; season with salt and pepper, to taste. Process until smooth and creamy. Add in the basil and use the "chop" setting until broken down. Then, puree until well mixed. With the motor running, add olive oil in a slow stream until well combined. Stop the machine and scrape down the sides of the food processor with a rubber spatula.

5. Place the cucumber noodles into a large bowl and add in the avocado pesto. Toss until cucumber noodles are well coated (you may need to cut them up!)

6. Divide the noodles between two plates, followed by the chicken and the blueberry salsa.

Nutrition Facts

Per serving | Calories: 320 | Fat: 12g | Carbohydrates: 24g | Fiber: 5.1g | Sugars: 14.5g | Protein: 30.2g |

Green Apple and Daikon Salad with Pepitas

Prep Time: 15 minutes

Cook Time: 10 minutes

Serves: 4

Ingredients:

- 2 daikon

- 1 granny smith apple

- 3 tablespoons avocado oil

- 3 tablespoons rice vinegar

- 2 tablespoons clementine juice

- 1 teaspoon lime juice

- 3 tablespoons fresh parsley, chopped

- 2 tablespoons pepitas, unsalted

Directions:

1. In a bowl, whisk together vinegar, juices, avocado oil and parsley.

2. Spiralize the daikon and green apple.

3. Toss the daikon and green apple gently to coat with dressing. Allow to sit for 5 minutes so the flavors blend. Sprinkle the pepitas on top and serve.

Nutrition Facts

Per serving | Calories: 181 | Fat: 11g | Carbohydrates: 14g | Fiber: 4g | Sugars: 9g | Protein: 2g |

Pesto Zoodles with Chicken Sausage

Prep Time: 10 minutes

Cook Time: 10 minutes

Serves: 5

Ingredients:

- 2 medium zucchini (4 cups noodles)

- 1 large yellow squash (3 cups noodles)

- 4 precooked chicken sausages, sliced into half-circles

- 5 tablespoons basil pesto

- ¼ teaspoon salt

- ¼ teaspoon ground pepper

Directions:

1. Start by creating noodles by running the zucchini and squash through a spiralizer. Place noodles in a large serving bowl.

2. Preheat a large nonstick skillet to medium-high heat. Add the sausages and cook, stirring, until they are brown on all sides and heated through.

3. Add the cooked sausage, basil pesto, salt and pepper to the noodles. Toss gently to coat. Serve.

Nutrition Facts

Per serving | Calories: 204.6 | Fat: 13.7g | Carbohydrates: 10.7g | Fiber: 3.2g | Sugars: 4.4g | Protein: 11.4g |

Spicy Shrimp and Asparagus over Zucchini Noodle Pasta

Prep Time: 10 minutes

Cook Time: 10-15 minutes

Serves: 2

Ingredients:

- 1 tablespoon olive or coconut oil

- 5 garlic cloves, minced

- 1 lb sliced asparagus

- ½ teaspoon sea salt

- 1 teaspoon crushed red pepper

- ¼ teaspoon freshly ground black pepper

- 2 medium zucchini, spiralized into noodles

- 1 lb shrimp, peeled and deveined

- 2 tablespoons of fresh lemon juice

- Chopped fresh parsley, for garnish

Directions:

1. Heat oil in a large nonstick skillet over medium heat. Add garlic, asparagus, salt, red pepper and black pepper; cook, stirring constantly, 2 to 3 minutes.

2. Add shrimp, and cook for 4 minutes, stirring frequently. Stir in lemon juice. Once shrimp looks cooked through, transfer the mixture to a plate; set aside.

3. In the same skillet, over medium heat, sauté the zucchini noodles for 1-2 minutes.

4. Place the shrimp and asparagus mixture back into the skillet. Give everything a stir to combine, then remove from heat. Sprinkle with fresh parsley and serve.

Nutrition Facts

Per serving | Calories: 326 | Fat: 8.54g | Carbohydrates: 14.67g | Fiber: 6.1g | Sugars: 5.04g | Protein: 52.31g |

Garlic Honey Chicken Carrot Noodles

Prep Time: 15 minutes

Cook Time: 25 minutes

Serves: 4

Ingredients:

- 1 pound boneless skinless chicken breasts, cut into bite sized pieces (roughly 1-1½" cubes)

- ½ cup cornstarch

- ½ teaspoon salt, plus more to taste

- ¼ teaspoon fresh cracked black pepper, plus more to taste

- ¼ cup + 1 tablespoon vegetable oil (you can substitute canola)

- 5-6 large carrots, peeled, ends trimmed & spiralized

- Red pepper flakes, crushed (to taste)

Sauce:

- 8 cloves garlic, minced

- 6 tablespoons reduced sodium soy sauce

- ½ cup honey

- ¼ cup sake

- ¼ cup fresh ginger, grated

- ⅛ teaspoon kosher salt

Garnish:

- ½ cup scallions, thinly sliced

- Sesame seeds (to taste)

Directions:

1. Preheat oven to 400°F and prepare an 8x11" baking pan with cooking spray.

2. *For the chicken*: in a large ziptop plastic bag, combine chicken pieces, cornstarch, salt and pepper.

   Seal bag; shake to coat chicken. Heat ¼ cup oil in a large sauté pan over medium-high heat. Add the chicken in batches so as not to overcrowd the pan. Cook the chicken on both sides until lightly browned, about 2-3 minutes (chicken will be raw on the inside). Transfer to prepared baking pan and spray the top of chicken with cooking spray. Bake in preheated oven for 15-20 minutes, or until cooked through.

3. *Meanwhile, prepare the noodles and sauce*: wipe the pan with a clean paper towel to remove any excess oil and reduce heat to medium high. Add 1 tablespoon clean oil to the pan. Add the carrot noodles and a pinch of red pepper flakes. Cook, stirring frequently, until softened, about 5 minutes. Season to taste with salt and pepper. Remove to a bowl and set aside.

4. Add minced garlic to the pan and stir until fragrant, less than 1 minute. Add the rest of the sauce ingredients and bring to a simmer, whisking occasionally. Simmer, stirring frequently, until thickened, about 3 to 5 minutes. Remove skillet from heat.

5. When the chicken pieces are cooked, remove them from the oven. Add the chicken to the pan with the sauce and toss to coat.

6. Serve chicken over carrot noodles. Garnish with sesame seeds, scallions and additional red pepper flakes.

Nutrition Facts

Per serving | Calories: 533 | Fat: 18g | Carbohydrates: 64g | Fiber: 3g | Sugars: 39g | Protein: 27g |

Bell Pepper Stuffed with Apple Tuna Salad

Prep Time: 5 minutes

Cook Time: 10-15 minutes

Serves: 4

Ingredients:

- 1 large Granny Smith apple

- 1 (5 oz) can tuna in water

- 2 packed cups of baby arugula

- ½ cup chopped celery

- 2 large red bell peppers

For the dressing:

- ⅔ cup + 2 tablespoons non-fat plain Greek Yogurt

- 1 tablespoon Dijon mustard

- 1 tablespoon lemon juice

- ½ teaspoon garlic powder

- Salt and pepper (to taste)

Directions:

1. Whisk together the yogurt, lemon juice, mustard, garlic powder, salt and pepper in a bowl. Set aside.

2. Slice the apple halfway lengthwise and spiralize it, using Blade B. Add the apple to a large bowl with the celery, tuna, arugula and dressing. Toss to combine thoroughly.

3. Slice the top off both the bell peppers and slice in half. Wash out the seeds and ribs (the white part inside).

4. Fill each half pepper with the apple tuna salad and serve.

Nutrition Facts

Per serving | Calories: 98 | Fat: 1g | Carbohydrates: 13g | Fiber: 3g | Sugars: 8g | Protein: 11g |

Pear Noodle, Shredded Kale and Brussels Sprouts Salad with Honey Dijon Vinaigrette

Prep Time: 10 minutes

Cook Time: 5-7 minutes

Serves: 4

Ingredients:

For the vinaigrette:

- 2 tablespoons apple cider vinegar

- 2 tablespoons extra virgin olive oil

- 1 teaspoon honey

- ½ teaspoon Dijon mustard

- 1 tablespoon minced shallot

- Salt and pepper (to taste)

For the salad:

- 6 oz (about 2 cups) Brussels sprouts, thinly sliced

- 1 pear, spiralized, Blade D (or Blade C), any pear will do — I love Bosc or Anjou

- 1 cup finely chopped (aka shredded) kale

- 3 tablespoons sliced blanched almonds

Directions:

1. Toast sliced almonds on a dry skillet over medium-high heat, tossing frequently until fragrant and golden, about 3 minutes. Set aside.

2. Whisk all the ingredients for the dressing together until well blended. Taste and adjust to your preference, then set aside.

3. In a large bowl, combine Brussels sprouts, pear noodles, toasted almonds, and kale. Pour over the vinaigrette and toss lightly to coat. Serve.

Nutrition Facts

Per serving | Calories: 157 | Fat: 11g | Carbohydrates: 15g | Fiber: 4g | Sugars: 7g | Protein: 4g |

Sweet Potato Noodles and Chicken Casserole

Prep Time: 10 minutes

Cook Time: 1 hour 45 minutes

Serves: 6

Ingredients:

- 1 lb boneless skinless chicken breast (or 12 oz shredded cooked chicken)

- 2 sweet potatoes (12 oz total), spiralized and cut into 6-inch lengths

- 4 medium vine tomatoes

- 4 dried guajillo chili peppers

- 1 teaspoon olive oil

- 4 garlic cloves

- 1 onion (quartered)

- ½ teaspoon cumin powder

- 1¼ teaspoons kosher salt

- ⅛ teaspoon black pepper

- 1 (15 oz) can black beans, rinsed and drained

- 1 cup frozen corn

- 5 oz pepper jack cheese

- Shredded chopped scallions for topping (optional)

Directions:

1. Preheat oven to 400°F.

2. Spiralize the sweet potatoes with the smallest noodle blade and place them in a 9 x 13 oval casserole dish.

3. If you're cooking the chicken, place the chicken breasts into a pot filled with 2 cups of water. Bring the water to a boil, then reduce it to a simmer. Cook chicken breasts for 10 minutes. Remove the chicken from water and let rest until cool enough to handle. Dice, slice, or shred as desired. Place in a large bowl.

4. Bring a large pot of water to boil. Add guajillos and reduce heat to a simmer. Cover and cook for about 15-20 minutes, or until softened. Remove peppers from water and let them cool. Remove stems, seeds, and membranes from peppers. Transfer to a blender.

5. Add 4 tomatoes to the same boiling water and cook 10 minutes. Remove with a slotted spoon and when cool enough to handle, peel off the skin. Transfer to the blender. Blend until smooth.

6. Meanwhile, in a medium skillet, heat the oil over medium-high heat. Add the onion and garlic and sauté until they become golden brown and caramelized. Transfer to the blender with the sauce along with cumin, salt, and pepper and blend well.

7. Pour the mixture into the large bowl with the shredded chicken, black beans and corn. Mix to combine.

8. Pour the mixture over the spiralized sweet potatoes, making sure the sauce mixes well and gets in between the spirals.

9. Top with pepper jack cheese, cover with aluminum foil and bake in preheated oven for 1 hour, or until the sweet potatoes are tender.

10. Top with scallions and serve.

Nutrition Facts

Per serving | Calories: 335 | Fat: 12g | Carbohydrates: 32g | Fiber: 6g | Sugars: 1g | Protein: 26g |

Chicken & Zoodles with Soy-Chili Sauce

Prep Time: 10 minutes

Cook Time: 15-20 minutes

Serves: 2

Ingredients:

- 6 oz skinless chicken breasts, cut into ½-inch pieces

- 2 medium zucchini, about 8 oz each, ends trimmed

- 1 teaspoon grapeseed or canola oil

- ½ red bell pepper, cut into ½-inch pieces

- Kosher salt and freshly ground black pepper (to taste)

- 1 teaspoon sesame oil

- 2 cloves garlic, minced

- 1 teaspoon fresh ground ginger

- 2 tablespoons crushed dry roasted peanuts

- 2 tablespoons thinly sliced scallions along diagonal

For the sauce:

- 1½ tablespoons reduced soy sauce (tamari for gluten free)

- 1 teaspoon hoisin sauce

- 1 tablespoon balsamic vinegar

- 2½ tablespoons water

- ½ tablespoon Sambal Oelek Red Chili Paste (or you can use Sriracha)

- 2 teaspoons cornstarch

- 2 teaspoons sugar

Directions:

1. Using a spiralizer with the thickest noodle blade, or a mandolin fitted with a julienne blade, cut the zucchini into

long spaghetti-like strips. If using a spiralizer, use kitchen scissors to cut the strands into pieces that are about 6 to 8 inches long so they're easier to eat.

2. Combine and whisk soy sauce, water, hoisin, balsamic, red chili paste (sriracha), sugar and cornstarch together in a small bowl; set aside.

3. Season chicken with salt and pepper, to taste. In large, deep nonstick pan or wok, heat oil over medium-high heat. Place chicken in pan and allow to cook for approximately 5 minutes, until browned and cooked through. Remove chicken from pot and set aside.

4. Reduce heat to medium, add sesame oil, ginger and garlic to the skillet and cook until fragrant, about 30 seconds. Add the bell pepper, stir in soy sauce mixture and bring to a boil; reduce heat and simmer until thickened and bubbling, about 1-2 minutes.

5. Add the spiralized zucchini and cook, tossing the noodles often in the sauce, until the zucchini just starts to soften, about 2 minutes. If it seems dry, don't worry, the zucchini will release moisture which helps create a sauce. Once cooked, mix in chicken and divide between 2 bowls (about 2 cups each).

6. Top with peanuts and scallions.

Nutrition Facts

Per serving | Calories: 277 | Fat: 12g | Carbohydrates: 21g | Fiber: 4g | Sugars: 9g | Protein: 24g |

Raw Spiralized Beet & Mandarin Salad with Mint

Prep Time: 5 minutes

Cook Time: 15 minutes

Serves: 2

Ingredients:

- 2 medium beets, ends trimmed

- 2 (4 oz) snack cups mandarin oranges, in juice

- 2 tablespoons red wine vinegar

- 1½ tablespoons olive oil

- 1 sprig mint, leaves torn

Directions:

1. When working with beets, wear rubber gloves to prevent your hands from getting dyed pink. Peel the beet and trim off the stem. Insert the thinner end into the round blade of the spiralizer, keeping it centered. Spiralize using the blade with the smallest triangles.Use kitchen scissors to cut strands if they are too long.

2. Drain the mandarin oranges, reserving 2 tablespoons juice.

3. In a medium bowl, whisk together the juice, red wine vinegar and olive oil. Add the beets and gently toss to coat evenly. Let it sit for 10 minutes.

4. Divide in 2 plates, top with mandarin oranges and mint.

Nutrition Facts

Per serving | Calories: 184 | Fat: 10g | Carbohydrates: 23g | Fiber: 2g | Sugars: 20g | Protein: 1g |

Spiralized Rutabaga with Tomatoes and Pesto

Prep Time: 5 minutes

Cook Time: 10 minutes

Serves: 2

Ingredients:

- 1-2 rutabagas, peeled (should make about 3 cups of noodles)

- 2 tablespoons red onion, chopped

- ½ tablespoon oil (avocado, coconut or olive oil will work)

- ⅓ cup Almond breeze unsweetened almond milk

- 2 tablespoons freshly prepared pesto

- ⅓ cup grape tomatoes, chopped

- Crushed red pepper (to taste)

Directions:

1. Use a spiralizer to make rutabaga "noodles".

2. Heat oil in a large skillet over medium-high heat. Add onion and sauté for about 2 minutes.

3. Add the rutabaga noodles and sauté for an additional 2 minutes.

4. Add almond milk, cook until noodles are tender but still crisp (about 3-4 minutes).

5. Stir in the pesto, tomatoes and crushed red pepper and toss to coat. Remove from heat and serve.

Nutrition Facts

Per serving | Calories: 167 | Fat: 9g | Carbohydrates: 20g | Fiber: 5g | Sugars: 11g | Protein: 4g |

Spiralized Butternut Squash Toast with Goat Cheese and Pomegranate Seeds

Prep Time: 5 minutes

Cook Time: 10 minutes

Serves: 2

Ingredients:

- 1 neck of butternut squash, peeled

- 2 slices cinnamon-raisin bread

- 1 ounce goat cheese

- ½ teaspoon ground cinnamon

- 1 teaspoon agave syrup

- 1 tablespoon pomegranate seeds

Directions:

1. Spiralize the butternut squash on largest grate.

2. Place butternut squash and ½ cup of water in a microwave-safe bowl. Cover tightly with microwavable plastic wrap and microwave 5 minutes, or until squash is slightly tender. Drain from water and let dry on a paper towel.

3. Toast the bread until it's golden brown and crisp on top. Divide goat cheese and spread onto each toast.

4. Lightly toss butternut squash with agave and sprinkle with cinnamon. Top each toast with squash. Sprinkle pomegranate seeds evenly over top. Serve.

Nutrition Facts

Per serving | Calories: 185 | Fat: 4.7g | Carbohydrates: 31g | Fiber: 4g | Protein: 7g |

Peanut and Daikon Radish Noodle Salad

Prep Time: 25 minutes

Cook Time: 10 minutes

Serves: 4

Ingredients:

For salad:

- 1 lb daikon radish

- 2 tablespoons lime juice

- 2 teaspoons peanut oil

- 1½ cups diced red pepper

- 1 (15 oz) can baby corn, drained and chopped

- 1½ cups frozen and shelled edamame, thawed

- ⅓ cup green onion, finely diced

- ⅓ cup cilantro, chopped

- ⅓ cup chopped peanuts

For dressing:

- ⅓ cup creamy peanut butter

- 3 tablespoons honey (or agave nectar if vegan)

- 2 tablespoons rice vinegar

- 2 tablespoons soy sauce or liquid aminos

- ¼ teaspoon salt

Directions:

1. Cut each daikon radish into half and spiralize it into spaghetti into a large bowl. Add 2 tablespoons lime juice and toss to coat. Refrigerate until you're ready to use.

2. Combine the dressing ingredients in a small bowl. Whisk to combine until creamy and thick; set aside.

3. Heat peanut oil in a pan over medium-high heat. Add edamame, red pepper, and baby corn to the pan and

cook for 3 minutes. Your vegetables should be lightly blackened, but not completely cooked through.

4. While your vegetables are cooking, toss daikon radish noodles with peanut dressing until thoroughly coated and then divide among 4 plates.

5. Top each plate of daikon noodles with the hot, stir-fried veggies. Sprinkle with chopped peanuts. Garnish with fresh green onions and cilantro. Serve warm.

Nutrition Facts

Per serving | Calories: 439 | Fat: 19g | Carbohydrates: 47.2g | Fiber: 12.7g | Sugars: 23.1g | Protein: 22.4g |

Spiralized Pear & Arugula Salad with Blue Cheese

Prep Time: 10 minutes

Cook Time: 5 minutes

Serves: 4

Ingredients:

Greek Yogurt Balsamic Dressing:

- ¼ cup nonfat plain Greek yogurt

- 3 tablespoons balsamic vinegar

- 1 tablespoon honey

- 1 teaspoon Dijon mustard

- Salt and pepper (to taste)

Salad:

- 2 Bosc or Anjou pears, spiralized into noodles

- 4-5 cups baby arugula (about 4½ ounces)

- ¾ cup walnuts

- ½ cup Wisconsin blue cheese, crumbled

Directions:

1. Mix the dressing ingredients in a bowl and whisk to combine thoroughly; set aside.

2. In another bowl, combine the pear noodles, walnuts, arugula and blue cheese.

3. Pour the dressing over salad just before serving and toss to combine.

Nutrition Facts

Per serving | Calories: 236 | Fat: 15g | Carbohydrates: 23g | Fiber: 4g | Sugars: 16g | Protein: 7g |

Cucumber Noodles & Melon Salad

Prep Time: 10 minutes

Cook Time: 5 minutes

Serves: 2

Ingredients:

For Cucumber Melon Salad:

- 2 cups cucumber noodles (using the $\frac{1}{8}$-inch noodle blade or Blade C)

- $1\frac{1}{2}$-2 cups mixed melon balls (cantelope, honeydew, crenshaw, etc); sizes of the melon balls can also be varied for visual interest

- Optional: Torn mint leaves to garnish

For Salad Dressing:

- $\frac{1}{4}$ cup freshly squeezed lime juice

- 2 tablespoon grape seed oil

- $1\frac{1}{2}$ teaspoons agave nectar

- 1 teaspoon fresh mint, diced

Directions:

1. Place cucumber noodles on the serving plates, 1 cup per plate. Add melon balls equally to each plate.

2. In a small bowl, whisk the dressing ingredients together until combined well. Lightly dress each salad. Garnish with torn mint leaves.

Nutrition Facts

Per serving | Calories: 210 | Fat: 14.07g | Carbohydrates: 21.95g | Fiber: 2.1g | Sugars: 17.8g | Protein: 1.94g |

One Pan Lemon Herb Salmon and Zoodles

Prep Time: 10 minutes

Cook Time: 30 minutes

Serves: 2

Ingredients:

- 2 medium zucchini, spiralized or chopped

- 2 (3-ounces) portions of salmon

- 1 tablespoon dried parsley

- 1 teaspoon Dijon mustard

- ¼ teaspoon rosemary

- ¼ teaspoon oregano

- ¼ teaspoon thyme

- 1 tablespoon minced garlic

- 1 tablespoon freshly squeezed lemon juice

- 1 teaspoon extra virgin olive oil

- Salt (to taste)

- Freshly ground black pepper (to taste)

- Sliced lemons for topping

Directions:

1. Preheat the oven to 350°F. Spray the 9x9 baking pan with cooking spray.

2. In a small bowl, combine the Dijon mustard, oil, thyme, rosemary, parsley, oregano and garlic. Whisk to combine.

3. Layer the spiralized zucchini on the bottom of the pan then place the salmon on top of the zucchini. Sprinkle with salt and freshly ground black pepper to taste.

4. Top fish with marinade, distributing it evenly between the fish and top with sliced lemons.

5. Place in the oven and bake at 350°F until fish is flaky and zucchini is tender, about 20-25 minutes.

6. Remove from oven and serve immediately.

Nutrition Facts

Per serving | Calories: 236 | Fat: 10.3g | Carbohydrates: 11.2g | Fiber: 3.6g | Sugars: 8.3g | Protein: 25.7g |

Broccoli Stem Noodles with Sesame Ginger Dressing

Prep Time: 5 minutes

Cook Time: 10 minutes

Serves: 4

Ingredients:

- 4 large broccoli stems

- 2 tablespoons toasted sesame oil

- 2 cloves garlic, minced

- 1 tablespoon coconut aminos or soy sauce

- 2 tablespoons apple cider vinegar

- 1 teaspoon grated ginger

- ⅛ teaspoon red pepper flakes

- ½ teaspoon salt

- ½ teaspoon pepper

- 2 tablespoons toasted sesame seeds

Directions:

1. Wash broccoli stems and trim ends. Spiralize the stems into noodles and place in a large mixing bowl.

2. Combine apple cider vinegar, coconut aminos (or soy sauce), sesame oil, garlic, salt, pepper, red pepper flakes and ginger in a small bowl.

3. Drizzle over noodles, toss to combine. Top dish with a sprinkling of sesame seeds.

4. Serve immediately.

Nutrition Facts

Per serving | Calories: 143 | Fat: 10.22g | Carbohydrates: 10.04g | Fiber: 3.62g | Sugars: 0.2g | Protein: 4.84g |

Haddock with Sesame Zoodles

Prep Time: 10 minutes

Cook Time: 15 minutes

Serves: 2

Ingredients:

- 2 fillets haddock

- 2 tablespoons avocado oil

- Salt and pepper (to taste)

- 2 large zucchini, spiralized (Blade C) or julienned

- 2 green onions, chopped

- ½ red cabbage, chopped or spiraled with Blade A

- Handful fresh cilantro, minced

- 1 tablespoon white sesame seeds

- 3 tablespoons soy sauce (or tamari)

- 1 tablespoon sesame oil

- 1 tablespoon rice vinegar

- 1 tablespoon agave nectar

Directions:

1. Preheat oven to 400°F.

2. Season the fish with some salt and pepper, and drizzle it with avocado oil. Place the haddock in the baking dish and bake in the preheated oven for 12 minutes.

3. Meanwhile, combine the zoodles, green onion, cilantro, sesame oil, cabbage, sesame seeds, rice vinegar, soy sauce, and agave nectar.

4. Toss to combine and let sit until fish is done cooking (you could also make this ahead of time and the zoodles will really absorb all the yummy flavors).

5. Finally, plate your zoodles and top with the piece of fish.

Nutrition Facts

Per serving | Calories: 374 | Fat: 11.3g | Carbohydrates: 26.8g | Fiber: 5.8g | Protein: 43.3g |

Carrot and Zucchini Noodles in Light Alfredo Sauce

Prep Time: 15 minutes

Cook Time: 15 minutes

Serves: 4

Ingredients:

For the Carrots and Zucchini Noodles:

- 4 zucchini, washed, dried and spiralized

- 3 large carrots, washed, dried and spiralized

- 3 tablespoons olive oil

- 1 pint cherry tomatoes, halved

- Salt and fresh ground pepper (to taste)

- 2 tablespoons sliced fresh basil

For the Light Alfredo Sauce:

- 1 tablespoon unsalted butter

- 2 cloves garlic, minced

- 2 teaspoons all-purpose flour

- 1 cup 2% milk

- ½ cup grated parmesan cheese, plus more for topping

- 2 tablespoons low-fat cream cheese

- Salt and fresh ground pepper (to taste)

Directions:

1. Heat a nonstick skillet over medium-high heat. Add olive oil and allow to heat.

2. Add the zucchini and carrot noodles and cook, stirring often, until slightly softened but still crunchy, about 5 minutes.

3. Add tomatoes and cook for an additional 2 minutes. Season with salt and pepper to taste. Remove from the heat, transfer to a colander and let drain at least 5 minutes.

4. In the meantime, prepare the alfredo sauce: melt the butter in a nonstick skillet over medium heat. Once butter is melted, add the garlic and cook for just one minute, until fragrant.

5. Add in the flour and cook, stirring with a wooden spoon for approximately 1 minute.

6. Whisk in the milk and cook, whisking constantly, until sauce begins to thicken, about 3 minutes.

7. Add the cream cheese and parmesan cheese and stir until melted.

8. Remove from heat and season with salt and pepper; taste for seasonings and adjust accordingly.

9. Transfer zucchini and carrot noodles to a plate or bowl and pour sauce on top.

10. Top with fresh basil and parmesan cheese.

Nutrition Facts

Per serving | Calories: 263 | Fat: 19.6g | Carbohydrates: 13g | Fiber: 2.3g | Sugars: 6.4g | Protein: 9.9g |

Garlicky Broccoli Noodles with Bacon

Prep Time: 10 minutes

Cook Time: 25-30 minutes

Serves: 4

Ingredients:

- 3 large broccoli crowns with stems

- 6 slices bacon

- 2 tablespoons olive oil

- Juice of 1 lemon and zest of ½ lemon

- ¼ teaspoon crushed red pepper

- 5 cloves garlic, thinly sliced

- 3 tablespoons grated Parmesan cheese

- Salt and pepper to taste

Directions:

1. Slice off the broccoli florets, taking as little stem as possible, and set aside. Then spiralize the stems into linguine.

2. Bring a deep saucepan filled halfway with salted water to a boil over high heat.

3. Add the broccoli florets and noodles to the boiling water and allow to boil for approximately 2 minutes or until easily pierced with a fork. Drain and pat dry.

4. Lightly coat a large skillet with cooking spray and heat to medium heat. When water flicked onto the skillet sizzles, add the bacon slices in an even layer, working in batches if needed. Cook for 3 minutes per side, or until the bacon is crisp and well browned. Remove bacon and set aside on a paper towel lined plate to drain, then crumble.

5. Wipe out the skillet with paper towels, return it to medium heat, and add the olive oil. When the oil is shimmering, add the broccoli noodles, broccoli florets, and crushed red pepper; season with salt and pepper. Cover and cook for 2 minutes, stirring occasionally.

6. Add the garlic, lemon zest and juice. Cover and cook for another 5 minutes, or until the broccoli is lightly browned.

7. Remove the pan from the heat. Stir in the cheese and gently toss to combine. Serve warm.

Nutrition Facts

Per serving | Calories: 194 | Fat: 13g | Carbohydrates: 13g | Fiber: 4g | Sugars: 3g | Protein: 10g |

You may also like

Smoothies are great for outdoor entertaining, summer bbqs, a nutritional breakfast, or just simply to quench your thirst. Loaded with fresh fruits and vegetables, these easy-to-make drinks will help you detox, beautify and energize in just minutes. These delicious drinks can be enjoyed in the morning, before or after a workout, or any time that you choose.

Find it on Amazon.com

https://www.amazon.com/dp/B0716D74ZF

Other books by Stephanie N. Collins You can find here

https://www.amazon.com/Stephanie-N-Collins/e/B01LZG40P9

Legal & Disclaimer

The information contained in this book is not designed to replace or take the place of any form of medicine or professional medical advice. The information in this book has been provided for educational and entertainment purposes only.

The information contained in this book has been compiled from sources deemed reliable, and it is accurate to the best of the Author's knowledge; however, the Author cannot guarantee its accuracy and validity and cannot be held liable for any errors or omissions. Changes are periodically made to this book. You must consult your doctor or get professional medical advice before using any of the suggested remedies, techniques, or information in this book.

Upon using the information contained in this book, you agree to hold harmless the Author from and against any damages, costs, and expenses, including any legal fees potentially resulting from the application of any of the information provided by this guide. This disclaimer applies to any damages or injury caused by the use and application, whether directly or indirectly, of any advice or information presented, whether for breach of contract, tort, negligence, personal injury, criminal intent, or under any other cause of action.

You agree to accept all risks of using the information presented inside this book. You need to consult a professional medical practitioner in order to ensure you are both able and healthy enough to participate in this program.

Made in the USA
Middletown, DE
15 November 2017